THE *Secret* OF THE LORD

THE *Secret* OF THE LORD
KEY TO YOUR DESTINY

BARBARA STICH

MAIDEN VOYAGE PUBLISHING
SAN FRANCISCO BAY AREA, CALIFORNIA

Unless otherwise noted, all Scriptures are taken from the New King James Version®. Copyright © 1982 by Thomas Nelson. Used by permission. All rights reserved.

Scripture quotations marked KJV are from the King James Version of the Bible. Public Domain.

Scripture quotations marked The Voice are copyright © 2012 Thomas Nelson, Inc. Used by permission. All rights reserved.

Scripture quotations marked (WNT) are taken from *Weymouth's New Testament in Modern Speech* by Richard Francis Weymouth. Harper & Row Publishers, Inc., New York, New York.

Scripture quotations marked AMP are taken from the Amplified Bible, © 1987 by the Zondervan Corporation. Used by permission. All rights reserved.

The Secret of the Lord – Key to Your Destiny
ISBN: 978-1-931545-08-2
Copyright © 2017 Ekklesia Productions
P. O. Box 2150, St. Augustine, FL 32085-2150

Published by Maiden Voyage Publishing
San Francisco Bay Area, California
dee.cartagena@gmail.com

Front and back cover images of gate, Filoli House & Gardens, Woodside, California, photographed by Deanne Cartagena. Filoli is a country estate set in 16 acres of formal gardens and surrounded by an additional 654 acres. Filoli was built for W. B. Bourn II between 1915 and 1917. The name of the estate is an acronym formed by combining the first two letters from the key words of Mr. Bourn's credo, "**Fi**ght for a just cause; **Lo**ve your fellow man; **Li**ve a good life."

Printed in the United States of America. All rights reserved under International Copyright Law. No part of this publication may be reproduced, stored in a retrieval system, or transmitted in any way by any means—electronic, mechanical, photocopy, recording, or otherwise—without the express written consent of the copyright holder.

Dedicated to the Bride of Christ

~With love

ENDORSEMENTS

The truths highlighted in *The Secret of the Lord – Key to Your Destiny* will cause the reader to shake off slumber and take their proper position in Christ.

This is a much needed message in this hour that, if received and heeded, will help prepare Christ's Bride—His glorious Church—for the Lord's return!

Bishop Bill Hamon (63 years of Ministry)
Bishop and Founder of Christian International
Apostolic Network
Santa Rosa Beach, FL

Author, *The Eternal Church, Birthing God's Purpose, The Day of the Saints,* and many others.

In *The Secret of the Lord – Key to Your Destiny*, Barbara has used scriptures and intertwined testimonies to prompt the reader to choose wisely and take their place on the Lord's side.

This book will set you on God's course for success and keep you on the path of victory for your life!

Dr. Chuck D. Pierce
President, Global Spheres, Inc.
President, Glory of Zion International Ministries
Corinth, TX

Dr. Pierce has authored over 20 books including *A Time to Triumph, Redeeming the Time,* and *Reordering Your Day.*

CONTENTS

Dedication

Introduction ix

CHAPTER 1 — 11
UNDERSTANDING THE FEAR OF THE LORD
Fear Defined
As He is, so are We...

CHAPTER 2 — 25
GOD'S PURIFYING FIRE
Where Wisdom Begins
The Sin of Pride
Removing Stumbling Blocks
Faith Works by Love
The Path of Humility

CHAPTER 3 — 41
EMBRACING THE NEW CREATION REALITY
A Walk of Obedience
Obedience is Better than Sacrifice
Fellowship and Forgiveness
Developing our Trust in God
Recognizing our Place
Total Commitment
Life-Giving Water

CHAPTER 4 — 65

TAKING THE HIGH ROAD: GOD'S RIGHTEOUS STANDARD

When Light Comes
What Does God Require of Us?
The Dangerous Place of Presumption
Walking in Newness of Life
A Revelation of Redemption
Put On the New Man
A Word on Praise

CHAPTER 5 — 89

THE BLESSINGS OF FEARING THE LORD

Thirty-Five Blessings to Meditate On

APPENDIX — 111

Becoming a Child of God
Receiving Power from On High
A Prayer of Consecration
My True Identity – A Confession

INTRODUCTION

"The secret of the Lord is with those who fear Him, and He will show them His covenant" (Psalm 25:14).

The word *secret*, *'cowd'* in Hebrew, is an interesting word in this Scripture. It is expressed 21 times in the Old Testament. The KJV Old Testament Hebrew Lexicon defines *'cowd'* as: council (of familiar conversation); circle (of familiar friends); assembly, company; counsel, secret counsel; familiar converse, intimacy (with God).

The Amplified Bible puts it this way: "The secret [of the sweet, satisfying companionship] of the Lord have they who fear (revere and worship) Him, and He will show them His covenant and reveal to them its [deep, inner] meaning" (see John 7:17; 15:15).

Sweet and satisfying companionship with the Lord — is that not our heart's desire? To know and love Him as we are known and loved by Him? Indeed, it is the inward longing of every heart. But this longing is not just sensed by us. God Himself is yearning for us to be at home in His presence!

Our gracious Father God purposed a life of blessing and fruitfulness for every one of us. As we position our hearts before Him, His love strengthens and sustains us, enabling us to fulfill *our* part of the covenant. In that place we truly come to know Him, even as we are known by Him.

This book is an expression of my quest to know the fear of the Lord and to describe the journey on the way. It is my heartfelt prayer that all of us will continue to be changed from glory to glory and fulfill all God has destined for us. We will walk in His secret counsel because we hold Him in reverential awe, our hearts are His, and He will continue to unfold His covenant to us.

Barbara Stich

St. Augustine, Florida
February 2017

My son, if you accept what I am telling you and
store My counsel and directives deep within you,
If you listen for Lady Wisdom, attune your ears to her,
and engage your mind to understand what she is telling you,
If you cry out to her for insight and beg for understanding,
If you sift through the clamor of everything around
you to seek her like some precious prize,
to search for her like buried treasure;

Then you will grasp what it means to truly respect
the Eternal, and you will have discovered the knowledge
of the one true God.

The Eternal is ready to share His wisdom with us,
for His words bring true knowledge and insight;
He has stored up the essentials of sound wisdom
For those who do right; He acts as a shield for those
who value integrity.

God protects the path of those who pursue justice,
watching over the lives of those who keep faith with Him.
With this wisdom you will be able to choose the
right road, seek justice, and decide what is good and fair
Because wisdom will penetrate deep within
and knowledge will become a good friend
to your soul.

Sound judgment will stand guard over you,
and understanding will watch over you
as the Lord promised.

—Proverbs 2:1–11, The Voice

CHAPTER 1

UNDERSTANDING THE FEAR OF THE LORD

> …There shall come forth a rod out of the stem of Jesse, and a Branch shall grow out of his roots:
> And the spirit of the Lord shall rest upon him, the spirit of wisdom and understanding, the spirit of counsel and might, the spirit of knowledge and of the fear of the Lord;
> And shall make him of quick understanding in the fear of the Lord: and he shall not judge after the sight of his eyes, neither reprove after the hearing of his ears:
> But with righteousness shall he judge the poor, and reprove with equity for the meek of the earth….
>
> Isaiah 11:1–4a

When I first came across this passage of Scripture decades ago, I rejoiced. Impulsively I thought, *Oh, how wonderful! I have found another gem in the treasure chest of God's Word!*

Beholding yet another facet of the Lord's mighty work of redemption, I gloated over the realization that because I was in Christ, the Spirit of the Lord rested upon *me!* The Spirit of wisdom and of understanding rested upon *me!* The Spirit of counsel and of might rested upon *me!* The Spirit of knowledge rested upon *me!*

I was quick to acknowledge ownership and claim this passage of Scripture as mine because I desired wisdom, understanding, counsel, might and knowledge.

But when I came to the end of verse 2, where the Spirit of the fear of the Lord is mentioned, I conveniently equated that with my initial decision to receive Jesus Christ as my Savior. I concluded that somehow in my acknowledging Jesus as Lord, I had demonstrated fear of the Lord.

I had read in the Bible that those who feared the Lord were the saints, and those who did not fear Him were, well, outsiders—not born again, not members of the household of faith. It was a very *natural* response to this Scripture. The Word of God went on to say in Isaiah 11:3a that He, ". . . shall make him of quick understanding in the fear of the Lord . . ." and I just thought, *That's right, the Holy Spirit will cause me to progressively understand the Lord and the salvation that He wrought for me.*

I am very glad that the One Who teaches us all things did not leave me in the dark! Thank God, He will be the Light to all who desire His illumination. *"The entrance of Your words gives light; it gives understanding to the simple"* (Psalm 119:130).

Fear Defined

In consulting Webster's Dictionary, we see that there are several meanings of the word *fear*. Some of the definitions are: 1) an unpleasant, often strong emotion caused by anticipation or awareness of danger; 2) an instance of, or state marked by, this emotion; 3) anxious concern; 4) profound reverence and awe, especially toward God.

In the Scriptures, Timothy identifies fear as a spirit. *"For God has not given us a spirit of fear, but of power and of love and of a sound mind"* (2 Timothy 1:7).

God did not give us the spirit of fear. There are many kinds of fear in the world which confront most everyone at one time or another, such as fear of failure, fear of rejection, fear of lack, fear of man, fear of the future, fear of some dreaded disease— it's a long list!

But God provides instructions for us which, if heeded, result in freedom from these kinds of fear. The only fear to embrace is the fear of the Lord. So in our context, fear must have a different meaning. Instead of negative ramifications, fear of the Lord must have desirable results.

Let's examine some of the negative fears we encounter and must resist.

Fear of failure is neither a facet of God's character nor a part of His vocabulary, and it should not be of His children. As a matter of fact, God declares "I will not fail you" over and over again to encourage His people as they are following Him.

Isaiah 41:10 states:

> Fear not, for I *am* with you; Be not dismayed, for I *am* your God. I will strengthen you, Yes, I will help you, I will uphold you with My righteous right hand.

There is nothing automatic about freedom from fear of failure, but if we continue in His Word and live by these eternal truths, we will be blessed, and fear of failure will not be part of our emotional makeup.

Declaration: Father, You say of Yourself that You do not change. What You did for Your people Israel thousands of years ago, You will do today. I thank You that You are with me indeed, and that You will strengthen, uphold, and help me at every turn because I trust and rely on You. Amen.

Fear of rejection is causing many today to embrace a philosophy or lifestyle at odds with godly values. Peer pressure, political correctness, the desire to belong and to be accepted demand a price no child of God ought to be willing to pay. The truth is that in Jesus Christ we have been accepted by God (see Ephesians 1:6), who had us in mind before the foundation of the world, anticipating the day that we would join His family and know His love and acceptance. No matter what we have done or have not done, regardless of our upbringing or choices, God's love says, "I forgive you; I accept you."

Declaration: Lord, You saw me from afar off – when as yet I did not see my need for You – and Your loving kindness and tender mercies drew me. Just like the father embraced the prodigal son in Luke 15, You received me with open arms. You put the robe of righteousness on me, placed a signet ring on my finger and sandals on my feet. You cleansed me, gave me authority and said, "Now go!" You are with me and for me, and I will do valiantly!

Lord, help me to see as You see in days ahead. When I meet someone who feels rejected, give me the words that will bring encouragement to that person. Use me to let them know how valuable and precious they are to You, and that You love them and have a good future in store for them. Amen.

Fear of lack or fear of poverty ought not be our experience when we live in obedience to God's Word. He is Jehovah-Jireh, our provider, isn't He?

The Book of Proverbs is a training manual on how to live. There are 31 chapters in Proverbs. A life-changing experience beckons us if we will meditate and digest these Scriptures. As we read a chapter a day, in only one month we will have entered into truth and wisdom with the power to renew our mind, strengthen our spirit, heal our bodies and change our lives!

The Book of Proverbs contains many examples of poverty coming on the disobedient, the stingy, the lazy, and those who don't bridle their tongue (see Proverbs 6:6–11; 10:4; 11:24; 13:18). We can open the door to poverty and lack in various ways, and these are a few of them.

On the other hand, the Word of God promises us that when we obey His Word, when we are diligent, when we are faithful with what the Lord has given us, and when we choose to make our mouths fountains of blessings, we will not lack any good thing (see Proverbs 12:24; 28:27; Matthew 24:45-47; 1 John 3:21, 22).

Galatians 6:7 says, *"Do not be deceived, God is not mocked; for whatever a man sows, that he will also reap."* We may not be aware of God's law of sowing and reaping, but it is true nonetheless and will work—for us or against us. The choice is ours. As our hearts become tuned to God's heart more and more and we submit to His leading, we will know how to prosper, and we will not lack any good thing.

Declaration: Lord, as I seek Your kingdom and Your righteousness first, all those things that I have need of will be added to me, according to Your Word in Matthew 6:33. I give my entire attention to what You are doing right now, and I choose to not get worked up over what may or may not happen tomorrow, trusting that You, Lord, will help me deal with whatever comes up in the future. Amen.

"**The fear of man** brings a snare, but whoever trusts in the Lord shall be safe" (Proverbs 29:25). Our trust must be in the Lord and His good intentions toward us. We cannot look to men for approval, because when our goal is to please men, we are not free to obey God's Word or even our own conscience and convictions. The apostles declared in Acts 5:29, "We ought to obey God rather than men."

Declaration: Psalm 119:89 declares that "forever, O Lord, Your word is settled in heaven." I encourage myself in You, Lord, by remembering Your Word and meditating on it. I let it fill my heart and mind until the truth overrides all other voices.

"In God I have put my trust; I will not be afraid. What can man do to me?" (Psalm 56:11)

"Let your conduct be without covetousness; be content with such things as you have. For He Himself has said, 'I will never leave you nor forsake you.' So we may boldly say: 'The Lord is my Helper; I will not fear. What can man do to me?' " (Hebrews 13:5, 6).

Fear or anxiety about the future is addressed lovingly by our Lord in Philippians 4:6, 7:

> Be anxious for nothing, but in everything by prayer and supplication, with thanksgiving, let your requests be made known to God;
> and the peace of God, which surpasses all understanding, will guard your hearts and minds through Christ Jesus.

I believe God meant what He said, don't you? He does not want us to fret or worry about anything because worry negates faith, and we cannot please God without faith. When we humbly position ourselves squarely on His Word (there is no better place to be!), He will lift us up at the right time. We cast all our anxieties upon Him, because "He cares for us affectionately and cares about us watchfully" (1 Peter 5:6, 7 AMP). Our mission each day is to demonstrate the Kingdom of God and His righteous standards, and in doing so, God is free to give us those things that we petitioned Him for (see Matthew 6:25-34).

We can enter into His rest knowing that He will undertake for us because we are in right standing with Him through the finished work of our Lord Jesus Christ.

Declaration: Lord, on those days that worry or anxiety about the future attempt to have a voice, I choose to believe Your Word. You made this awesome promise in Isaiah 46:4, and I receive it and take my rest in it. You said, "Even when you are old I will be the same, and when you are grey-haired I will take care of you: I will still be responsible for what I made; yes, I will take you and keep you safe" (Bible in Basic English).

We don't have to fear diseases because *"He Himself took our infirmities and bore our sicknesses"* so we don't have to carry them (Matthew 8:17). Jesus showed us the Father's attitude toward sickness when He *"went about doing good and healing all who were oppressed by the devil, for God was with Him"* (Acts 10:38). God says of Himself that He changes not, that He is no respecter of persons, and that His Word is forever settled in heaven (Malachi 3:6; Hebrews 13:8; Acts 10:34; Psalm 119:89).

From these examples, the conclusion must be drawn that we are not to fear, be intimidated or terrorized by people or situations. Therefore, we can lay aside Webster's first three definitions for *fear* as not applicable—indeed, inappropriate. Our conclusion then is that the last definition of fear, meaning *a profound reverence and awe*, is how we are to live our lives before God. We are not to be afraid or in terror of Him, but we are to show reverential fear and awe toward Him.

In the following Scriptures the Lord Jesus enjoins us to do exactly that:

> Whatever I tell you in the dark, speak in the light, and what you hear in the ear, preach on the housetops.
> And do not fear those who kill the body but cannot kill the soul. But rather fear Him who is able to destroy both soul and body in hell.
> Matthew 10:27, 28

So we see that the Word of God is very specific about whom to fear, and with what kind of actions to give expression to that reverential fear.

As He is, so are We

Jesus said that a servant is not greater than his master (John 13:16). Have you noticed that our Master, the Lord Jesus, does not ask us to do anything that He has not done also?

> Who [Jesus] in the days of His flesh, when He had offered up prayers and supplications, with vehement cries and tears to Him who was able to save Him from death, and was heard because of His godly fear,
> though He was a Son, yet He learned obedience by the things which He suffered.
> And having been perfected, He became the author of eternal salvation to all who obey Him.
> Hebrews 5:7–9

What an eye-opening statement! There was no question about His relationship with Father God. Jesus was (and is, and ever shall be) His Son. Yet, the Scripture says He learned obedience through the things He suffered. This is the example of obedience Jesus left for us to follow!

So what exactly did Jesus suffer while He was among men? We know it couldn't have been sickness or disease, because the Word of God says in I John 3:8 that He came to destroy the works of the devil. In Acts 10:38 we read that He went about healing all that were oppressed of the devil. So we know He didn't learn obedience by being sick, because wherever He went, He brought healing if the people would receive it.

We know it couldn't have been the unkind, detestable, ugly things people said about Him that perfected His obedience. If it was true that He learned obedience through unkind, ugly words and actions by others, every one of us would also be obedient, because we all have been treated unkindly by people at one time or another.

Apart from the ultimate act of obedience of laying down His life, I believe Jesus learned obedience by responding to provocations and testings the way God His Father desired. Jesus said of Himself that He always did those things He saw His Father do (see John 5:19). Not only did He bring healing to the sick, deliverance to the oppressed and prosperity to the poor, He also spoke the truth in love, blessed those who cursed Him, and forgave those who trespassed against Him. He reviled not again when He was reviled, neither was any deceitful language heard from His mouth.

He judged by the standard of God. The Word declares that the scepter of righteousness is the scepter of His Kingdom. Jesus did not have one standard during His earthly life but now has a different one. No, it's the same standard, the same rule, the same weights, the same measure, the same balance. God does not have two different balances; He Himself declares that double standards are an abomination to Him (Proverbs 11:1). He never changes. He is still the same as He was 2,000 years ago when He walked this earth, and He will be the same for all eternity.

What He hated and abhorred in Moses' day He hates and abhors today. What He called sin in Jesus' day is still sin today. Jesus is called the chief cornerstone, the one that all the other "living stones" — that's us — are fitted to.

Imagine, if you will, a county courthouse. Let's say it was built in the style of the Renaissance — it's an imposing structure. In your mind's eye pick out the cornerstone. Now imagine that stone changing shapes! What is happening? The changing shape of the cornerstone is affecting the position of every other stone in the building, and shortly the entire structure lies in ruins.

You can see how absurd it is to think that God would divert even one iota from the declarations He made about Himself. It's inconceivable. He does not change! He would be defeating His own purpose if He did. As a matter of fact, Jesus said in one place that "a house divided against itself cannot stand" (Luke 11:17). If we want to function in that house, that building of the Lord which is fitly joined together and strengthened by that which every joint supplies, (did you know you were a joint?) we will have to lay aside our own ideas and submit ourselves to Holy Spirit, the Teacher of the Church. He knows the lesson plan for each student—He designed the curriculum. He knows best which class we need to be taking because He knows the entire plan of God—His whole counsel.

In Matthew 22:14 we read, ". . . many are called, but few are chosen." That is so not because God desired and decreed it; it is so because only few prove themselves to be chosen ones. Only a few are willing to purge themselves and become vessels of honor, fit for the Master's use (2 Timothy 2:21). The Scripture says, *"Let everyone that names the name of Christ depart from iniquity"* (2 Timothy 2:19). The word *let* implies an action or response on *our* part!

It is so simple to find God's will for you: Just sell out to Him. Be a person of integrity so that you and others can have faith in your word. Mean what you say and keep your promise. To the degree that we are true to our word, the Word of God will be true to us. The Father's heart is longing for us to take our rightful place in this earth. Let's offer this prayer to Him right here.

> *To the degree that we are true to our word, the Word of God will be true to us.*

Prayer: Lord, forgive me where I have not obeyed You fully. I really want to be in the center of Your will. I want to be all You have destined me to be. Please strengthen me where I need it. Give me the grace to forgive myself and others. Give me new vision for the road ahead. Make me a blessing. Amen.

CHAPTER 2

GOD'S PURIFYING FIRE

> Therefore, since we are receiving a kingdom which cannot be shaken, let us have grace, by which we may serve God acceptably with reverence and godly fear. For our God is a consuming fire.
>
> Hebrews 12:28, 29

The fear of the Lord and the fire of God go hand-in-hand. When we walk in the fear of the Lord, we submit ourselves to the fire of the Lord. It is our desire to get rid of anything in our lives that is displeasing to Him.

We can express the manifestation of God's power and God's presence in various emotions. We can experience Him in unspeakable thanksgiving and be overwhelmed by His great goodness. We know Him as the Lover of our soul; the One Who satisfies every part of our being so that indeed we know we are complete in Him. We give Him honor and praise, worshipping Him Who is the Almighty God, Creator of the universe — our Father.

The emotions and feelings we experience with God are good, but there is something that we need to release ourselves to in the Body of Christ; it is not an emotion—it is a heart stance: the reverential fear of God.

When we go about our daily business, do we recognize the fact that God, by His Spirit, is right there with us? And if we do recognize this, is it influencing our attitude, our behavior, in any way? Are we paying due respect to the Lord, knowing His Word and how He feels about a certain issue?

Let's say we are travelling in our car down the freeway, flowing with the traffic, which in some places means about ten miles above the speed limit. Suddenly all the cars in front of us reduce speed, and we do, too. Moments later we come around the bend, and there is the reason for the slowdown: a highway patrol car. When the drivers in front of us saw it sitting by the side of the road, they immediately took their foot off the gas pedal; it almost was a reflex.

Now they did that—and we do that—because we recognize that's *the law*. The highway patrol is an authority ordained by God, according to Romans 13, and we respect them by obeying the rules governing freeway traffic.

Where Wisdom Begins

How much more must we respect and honor God Who is *the* Lawgiver! All good judgment, all sound rules and practices proceed from the Father and honor the King of kings who fulfilled the Law. Wise men have produced laws and rules and ordinances which are good, just, and sound, but people aren't born with that kind of wisdom. Proverbs 9:10 declares that the fear of the Lord is the beginning of wisdom.

In Philippians 2:12 we read that we should work out our own salvation with fear and trembling, not any way we see fit. So we look to Jesus who demonstrated to us a life submitted and yielded to the Father.

The Scripture continues: *"**For it is God** who works in you both to will and to do for His good pleasure. Do all things without complaining and disputing, that you may become blameless and harmless, children of God without fault in the midst of a crooked and perverse generation, among whom you shine as lights in the world, holding fast the word of life . . . "* (Philippians 2:13–16).

Yes, God loves us. Yes, He is forever for us, His saving arm is outstretched toward all who call on Him. But call to mind a portion of Scripture that stands just as sure and unchangeable today as it did when the Apostle Paul penned it by the Holy Spirit to the saints at Rome almost 2,000 years ago.

> . . . Do not be haughty, but fear.
> For if God did not spare the natural branches, He may not spare you either.
> Therefore consider the goodness and severity of God: on those who fell, severity, but toward you, goodness, if you continue in His goodness.
> Otherwise you also will be cut off.
>
> Romans 11:20–22

Paul was speaking here of the natural branches, Israel, those who were cut off from the olive tree because of their unbelief, their disobedience. Paul said in the verse previous that it was by faith in Jesus that we were grafted in.

How many times in the Old Testament did the Lord command the children of Israel to fear Him, to obey Him, to keep His commandments?! I believe the Spirit of God is speaking to us today with the same fervency, the same urgency:

> And do this, knowing the time, that now it is high time to awake out of sleep; for now our salvation is nearer than when we first believed.
> The night is far spent, the day is at hand. Therefore let us cast off the works of darkness, and let us put on the armor of light.
> Let us walk properly, as in the day, not in revelry and drunkenness, not in lewdness and lust, not in strife and envy.
> But put on the Lord Jesus Christ, and make no provision for the flesh, to fulfill its lusts.
> Romans 13:11-14

When John the Baptist preached repentance in the wilderness of Judaea, the Bible says that Jerusalem, all Judaea, and all the region round about Jordan went out to him, and all were baptized by him in the River Jordan, confessing their sins. He said,

> "I indeed baptize you with water unto repentance, but He who is coming after me is mightier than I, whose sandals I am not worthy to carry. He will baptize you with the Holy Spirit and fire.
> "His winnowing fan is in His hand, and He will thoroughly clean out His threshing floor, and gather His wheat into the barn; but He will burn up the chaff with unquenchable fire."
> Matthew 3:11-12

The fire of God, the revelation He grants us, has one purpose: to make us more like Him. This is for *our* benefit as much as it is for His Kingdom!

In this process, it becomes necessary for us to let go of those things that are clinging to us from our old nature. We cannot say we want to walk like Jesus and do the greater works but live our lives as we did before we knew Him as our Savior. If we truly want to represent Him well, we should imitate Him — which requires that we become intimately acquainted with Him.

It is said that the best time to meet with the Lord is at the beginning of each day. Whether we pray, meditate, or praise Him, let us allow Him to knit our hearts to His. He will not fail to reveal His heart of love to us and we in turn will reflect Him more and more.

Prayer: Father, I want to be all You created me to be. Today I let go of my limited way of perceiving situations and people, and even myself. I let go of pre-judging anything and anyone. In its place, I receive Your wisdom, Your plans and purposes. The potential You placed in me can now flourish because I submit myself to You — spirit, soul and body. Thank You for keeping me and causing me to stand in the days ahead. Amen.

The Sin of Pride

Jesus came to reveal the Father to us—His personality, His character, His nature, His attitude. For instance, Jesus was meek and lowly in heart (Matthew 11:29). There wasn't a trace of pride in Him. He didn't seek to sit at the head table; the very fact that He was sent from God placed Him—figuratively—at the center of the head table wherever He happened to be sitting.

Pride is a sin. God hates pride. Pride cost Lucifer his exalted position in heaven. It cost him God's presence. A humble and contrite heart has gained victory over the prideful notions that some rules or laws, whether spiritual or natural, don't apply to us, or that our own sufficiency or excellence is enough.

Pride cost Satan his position and God's presence.

"For thus says the High and Lofty One Who inhabits eternity, whose name is Holy: 'I dwell in the high and holy place with him who has a contrite and humble spirit, to revive the spirit of the humble, and to revive the heart of the contrite ones'" (Isaiah 57:15).

The Lord says that right there, in His high and holy place, He keeps company with those who recognize their condition, are repentant over it, and assume the position of humility. They are the ones who submit out of reverence to the Greater One. And then the Lord declares that He will make alive again their spirits and hearts. How wonderful, how marvelous, how encouraging and motivating this is for all of us!

When we miss the mark, Holy Spirit will convict us. It is important to remember God's point of view: He will always—

always — always be the Redeemer, the Life Giver, the One who saves and heals. When He convicts us and we acknowledge and receive it, it will bring us closer to Him; we are drawn by His love and goodness. The Lord knows how to redeem every situation and every person!

Conviction vs. Condemnation

The opposite of conviction is condemnation, and it is brought on by the enemy of our soul, the accuser. We've all felt it. Condemnation brings with it the loathing of self and of hopelessness — of having forfeited our place — and it takes us away from the Lord. Beloved, every single one of us is a work in progress! We need to distinguish between how *we* see versus how *God* sees. The Word of God squarely declares that there is NO condemnation to those in Christ Jesus whose walk is upright. Let's embrace His Word which is life and health and not waste energy on a point of view that does not line up with the Word of God. Let's stay focused on what HE has done for us and who HE has called us to be.

Prayer: Lord, I am so thankful that I belong to You, and that You open my eyes to see the way You see. Teach me to love what You love and hate what You hate. I declare with King David from Psalm 40:1-3: "I waited patiently for the Lord; and He inclined to me, and heard my cry. He also brought me up out of a horrible pit, out of the miry clay, and set my feet upon a rock, and established my steps. He has put a new song in my mouth — praise to our God; many will see it and fear, and will trust in the Lord." Amen.

Removing Stumbling Blocks

Romans 11:29 says, *"For the gifts and the calling of God are irrevocable."* Some of us interpret that to mean that God's anointing—His expression through us—will abide on a person regardless of his or her lifestyle. That is not so. The way we conduct ourselves will either hinder God's work through us or enhance it.

There is another verse in the Bible which says, *". . . to whom much is given, from him much will be required"* (Luke 12:48). God has provided absolutely no slack for anyone in the Body of Christ, be they minister or layman. The one in public ministry has a greater responsibility because of higher visibility—his life affects so many more people.

The Apostle Paul exhorts the Corinthians to ". . . imitate me, watch my ways, follow my example, just as I, too, always seek to imitate the Anointed One" (1 Corinthians 11:1, The Voice).

The temptation is there to let our lower nature rule when we observe people in positions of leadership missing the mark. Some of us may think, *If it's okay for them, it must be okay for me,* but nothing could be further from the truth. What we tolerate and what we compromise will have a profound effect down the road, be it in one month, one year, or ten years. In the natural, think about your journey being off course by just one degree. The further out you go from the point of origin, the wider the gap will be between your goal and where you end up.

The Apostle Peter said the following in this letter to the Church:

> His divine power has given us everything we need to experience life and to reflect God's true nature *through the knowledge of the One* who called us by His glory and virtue.
> Through these things, we have received God's great and valuable promises, so we might escape the corruption of worldly desires and share in the divine nature.
>
> 2 Peter 1:3-4 (The Voice)

Jesus, the Living Word, desires for us to really, really know Him—not know *about* Him. We can do nothing apart from Him. John 15: 5-8, clearly shows us the One Who is at work in us, and Who deserves all the glory for anything accomplished through us. Jesus says: *"I am the vine, you are the branches. He who abides in Me, and I in him, bears much fruit; for without Me you can do nothing…. If you abide in Me, and My words abide in you, you will ask what you desire, and it shall be done for you. By this My Father is glorified, that you bear much fruit; so you will be My disciples."*

There comes a joy and renewed strength in God when we grasp just how much He loves us and is committed to our success. Once we see clearly what He requires of us, don't we want to obey Him with all our heart? Yes, we do!

Let us be willing to receive the correction and instruction of the Lord:

> "For whom the Lord loves He chastens,
> And scourges every son whom He receives."
> If you endure chastening, God deals with you as with sons; for what son is there whom a father does not chasten?
>
> Hebrews 12:6, 7

In Hebrews 12:8 we read further that *all* are experiencing the correction of the Lord. And why does the Lord do this? Verse 10 shows us He does it for our profit so that we would be positioned to share in His holiness. Verse 14 goes on to say, *"Pursue peace with all people, and holiness, without which no one will see the Lord. . . ."* Yet it is obvious not all of us have been determined enough to profit from His correction. Let us submit to the Lord and allow Him to do any work in us necessary to bring us to the place where we are free from any weight or sin that would hinder our fellowship with Him, and where we are of most benefit to Him and His Kingdom. Jesus said to His disciples (disciplined followers) in Matthew 11:29: *"Take My yoke upon you and learn from Me, for I am gentle and lowly in heart, and you will find rest for your souls."* His yoke is easy, and His burden is light. Many times we have such a difficult season because we won't take His yoke. He will not put it on us; we have to do it.

Some of us want the power of the Holy Spirit, but we don't want the fire that comes with it. John the Baptist said that Jesus would baptize us with the Holy Ghost *and* with fire. God will not be able to work through us to the extent of the giftings He placed within us if we, who are commanded to present our bodies a living sacrifice, holy and acceptable to God, keep shrinking back. There is no victory without a battle. There is no gold without refining fire. We might consider looking at conflict as another opportunity to prove that indeed we reign in this life by Jesus Christ our Lord, the Supreme Ruler of the universe. Are we in Him? Is He in us? Then all things are under our feet! Let's believe it, act on it, and demonstrate it. He has given to everyone the measure of faith. But remember, faith works by love (Galatians 5:6b).

Prayer: Lord, You know! You know every hard place I have been in, and You know how I got into these hard places, these difficult situations. Please forgive me for ignoring Your leading – Your still, small voice. I want to live in harmony, wholeness and strength with You and the people in my life. Open my ears to hear You more clearly. I will do my part and close my ear gate to everything that opposes You. I will rehearse Your Word which infuses me with Your life and strength so I won't stumble or fall. Amen.

Faith Works by Love

Love is neither an emotion nor a feeling; it is an outward expression of an inward decision. Love is divine. God's love for us and in us is perfect.

The Apostle Paul describes the kind of love we have received and should function in.

First Corinthians 13 says this:

> *Love is neither an emotion nor a feeling; it is an outward expression of an inward decision.*

> If I speak in the tongues of men and even of angels, but have not love (that reasoning, intentional, spiritual devotion such as is inspired by God's love for and in us), I am only a noisy gong or a clanging cymbal.

And if I have prophetic powers (the gift of interpreting the divine will and purpose), and understand all the secret truths and mysteries and possess all knowledge, and if I have sufficient faith so that I can remove mountains, but have not love (God's love in me) I am nothing (a useless nobody).

Even if I dole out all that I have [to the poor in providing] food, and if I surrender my body to be burned or in order that I may glory, but have not love (God's love in me), I gain nothing.

Love endures long and is patient and kind; love never is envious nor boils over with jealousy, is not boastful or vainglorious, does not display itself haughtily.

It is not conceited (arrogant and inflated with pride); it is not rude (unmannerly) and does not act unbecomingly. Love (God's love in us) does not insist on its own rights or its own way, for it is not self-seeking; it is not touchy or fretful or resentful; it takes no account of the evil done to it, it pays no attention to a suffered wrong.

It does not rejoice at injustice and unrighteousness, but rejoices when right and truth prevail.

Love bears up under anything and everything that comes, is ever ready to believe the best of every person, its hopes are fadeless under all circumstances, and it endures everything without weakening.

Love never fails [never fades out or becomes obsolete or comes to an end]. As for prophecy (the gift of interpreting the divine will and purpose), it will be fulfilled and pass away; as for tongues, they will be destroyed and cease; as for knowledge, it will pass away, it will lose its value and be superseded by truth.

For our knowledge is fragmentary (incomplete and imperfect), and our

> prophecy (our teaching) is fragmentary (incomplete and imperfect).
> But when the complete and perfect (total) comes, the incomplete and imperfect will vanish away (become antiquated, void, and superseded).
> When I was a child, I talked like a child, I thought like a child, I reasoned like a child; now that I have become a man, I am done with childish ways and have put them aside.
> For now we are looking in a mirror that gives only a dim (blurred) reflection of reality as in a riddle or enigma, but then when perfection comes we shall see in reality and face to face! Now I know in part (imperfectly), but then I shall know and understand fully and clearly, even in the same manner as I have been fully and clearly known and understood by God.
> And so faith, hope, love abide, faith — conviction and belief respecting man's relation to God and divine things; hope — joyful and confident expectation of eternal salvation; love — true affection for God and man, growing out of God's love for and in us, these three; but the greatest of these is love.
>
> 1 Corinthians 13:1-13, AMP

The motivation for anything we undertake for God must be love. Just as it was Jesus' purpose to show us the Father and to do His will, *God's* plans and purposes must be our goal. In the Body of Christ we have this issue: doing those things that are right and good but *not* what God has called and equipped us to do individually.

Do you know there are many of us today doing *good* things in the name of the Lord who will not receive a reward for those works because that is not what *God* asked us to do? We do what seems good to *us*...what we have seen someone else do... what *we think* is ministry. We must stop walking in our own wisdom and not place *our* traditions, opinions and desires above God's will for us. Those are some of the high things that exalt themselves against the knowledge of God, and the Word tells us to pull them down by bringing them into subjection to the Spirit of God:

> For the weapons of our warfare are not carnal but mighty in God for pulling down strongholds,
> casting down arguments and every high thing that exalts itself against the knowledge of God, bringing every thought into captivity to the obedience of Christ....
>
> 2 Corinthians 10:4, 5

I believe that the Bride of Christ will come to the full, clear, deep understanding of what the Lord requires of her and pursue that with all determination, always motivated by the love of God.

Prayer: Father, please forgive me for every time I followed my own wisdom and desire, believing it was good and acceptable in Your sight. I pray with the Psalmist David who said, "Who can understand his errors? Cleanse me from secret faults. Keep back Your servant also from presumptuous sins; let them not have dominion over me. Then I shall be blameless, and I shall be innocent of great transgression"

(Psalm 19:12, 13). Lord, I ask You to show me where I have insisted on my own way. I will rely on the grace You have already given me to choose Your way. However noble I think my works of faith are, today I acknowledge that apart from Your divine love they don't receive Your approval. Motivate my faith by Your love, and so enable me to be an effective member of Your household of faith. Amen.

The Path of Humility

The prophet Micah gave us some plain words, easy to be understood, when he said, *"He has told you, mortals, what is good in His sight. What else does the Eternal ask of you but to live justly and to love kindness and to walk with your True God in all humility?"* (Micah 6:8, The Voice).

Humility will choose God's ways; and so we look to Jesus, the author and finisher of our faith. He demonstrated for us how to live.

Humility will choose God's ways....

Solomon knew how to walk in humility. In Proverbs 8:33 we read, *"The fear of the Lord is to hate evil; pride and arrogance [the opposite of humility] and the evil way and the perverse or disobedient mouth I hate."*

He repeated it in Proverbs 3:7 where he said, *"Do not be wise [proud and arrogant] in your own eyes; fear the Lord and depart from evil."*

His father David set a good example in that regard. Psalm 101 gives us insight into David's heart:

> I will sing of God's unsparing love and justice; to You, O Eternal One, I will sing praises.
> I will seek to live a life of integrity; when will You come to me? I will walk in my house with an honest and true heart.
> I will refuse to look on any sordid thing; I detest the worthless deeds of those who stray; evil will not get a hold on me.
> I will rid my heart of all perversion; I will not flirt with any evil.
>
> Psalm 101:1–4, The Voice

Prayer: Lord, how honored and privileged I am to carry Your presence! I desire to live in such harmony with You that You are magnified in all I think, say and do. My heart is fixed on You, Lord. My mind is stayed on You. I look to You, Jesus, and I invite You to express Yourself through me in miraculous, wondrous, world-changing ways! I acknowledge that every good work I co-labor with You in is on the basis of Your shed blood. You alone deserve all the honor and glory, Jesus! Amen!

CHAPTER 3

Embracing the New Creation Reality

> His delight is in the fear of the Lord, and He shall not judge by the sight of His eyes, nor decide by the hearing of His ears.
>
> Isaiah 11:3

This prophetic passage describes the coming Redeemer and tells us that He will not be led by His physical senses, that He will not be ruled by His body. Instead, He will judge with righteousness, which is the standard of God, and which God imparts to us who meet one condition: We must be born again.

When we are born again and have joined the family of God, we have immediate, certain rights because of our new relationship with our Heavenly Father. Before, we were separated from God because of sin, but now we are alive in Him and adopted into His family, giving us the opportunity to draw our very life from the source of all life—God Himself.

We were alienated from God, without hope in the world; but now we have been brought near by the blood of the Lamb of God (see Ephesians 2:13).

We once walked in darkness, but now we are called children of light by the same One Who translated us into the Kingdom of light (see Colossians 1:13). A real change has taken place in our spiritual condition and position, and God expects us to walk in this new life He has secured for us. He paid the highest price to redeem us, to buy us back. He desires for His children to be holy—set apart—for He is holy. He wants us to have His mind, His faith, His strength, His peace, His joy. He has made His abundance available to us, yet the family of God seems to be sorely lacking on so many counts.

A Walk of Obedience

The reason for this spiritual poverty can be summed up in one word: disobedience. This disobedience is usually not the kind that is overtly antagonistic toward authority. It is much more subtle. At its root, I believe, is insufficient information about the personhood of God—being only casually acquainted with Him.

God has not been thought important enough or fascinating enough by many of us, and so we have not made an effort to really get to know Him. With our hearts and minds we have been everywhere but the Throne Room, and this works to our great detriment. For many of us it is high time that we paid Him an extended visit!

We have experienced His forgiveness, His mercy and His compassion, but we must also get to know His holiness, His glorious presence, the sacredness of His closeness in a profound and lasting way.

Let's identify from the following Scripture where many of us are in our walk with the Lord today:

> Simon Peter, a bondservant and apostle of Jesus Christ, to those who have obtained like precious faith with us by the righteousness of our God and Savior Jesus Christ [that includes us!]:
> Grace and peace be multiplied to you in the knowledge of God and of Jesus our Lord,
> as His divine power has given to us all things that pertain to life and godliness, through the knowledge of Him who called us by glory and virtue,
> By which have been given to us exceedingly great and precious promises, that through these you may be partakers of the divine nature, having escaped the corruption that is in the world through lust.
>
> 2 Peter 1:1-4

Some of us have stopped right here and not gone one step further. We are thrilled over the fact that we have become partakers of God's nature; that we have been forgiven and God has removed our sins as far as the east is from the west; that we are joint-heirs with Christ; that we have been raised up with Him and now are seated with Him in heavenly places. It is true that we are more than conquerors because the One in us is greater than any adversary in the world.

Our God-given ability to be imaginative has envisioned all these wonderful truths, and indeed it is important to see ourselves in that way.

However, the Church has been selective in employing that imagery. How many of us have identified with Jesus Christ in His godliness and virtue? In His patience? His love? His mercy and compassion?

Verses 1 through 4 inform us of what God freely bestowed upon us at the New Birth. No action or deed of ours could have caused any of these things to come to pass in our lives. We had to receive them all by faith in God—faith in His love, faith in His grace, faith in His Word.

Notice, too, that according to verse 2, it is through the knowledge of God and of Jesus our Lord that "grace and peace are multiplied to us." They don't come any other way.

> ...it is through the knowledge of God and of Jesus our Lord that grace and peace are multiplied to us.

It stands to reason, then, that the more revelation knowledge we have *and apply to the way we conduct ourselves*, the more grace and peace are multiplied to us. God does not want us to be lopsided in anything.

The Apostle Peter, in admonishing the Church, went on to say by the Holy Spirit:

> But also for this very reason, *giving all diligence,* add to your faith virtue, to virtue knowledge,
> to knowledge self-control, to self-control perseverance, to perseverance godliness,
> to godliness brotherly kindness, and to brotherly kindness love.
> For if these things are yours and abound, you will be neither barren nor unfruitful in the knowledge of our Lord Jesus Christ.
> For he who lacks these things is shortsighted, even to blindness, and has forgotten that he was cleansed from his old sins.
> Therefore, brethren, *be even more diligent to make* your call and election *sure,* for if you do these things you will never stumble.
>
> 2 Peter 1:5–10

I have emphasized certain phrases in this passage to illustrate a point. You see, God has done His part, but there are things *we* must do! Virtue is acquired! *We* add to our faith virtue!

The disciple of the Lord understands that verses 5 through 10 do not list options or suggestions, but character traits that need to be worked out in this new creation—the creature that has been given those exceeding great and precious promises in order to reflect the divine nature.

I want you to notice that there isn't a single "maybe", "if you think you can do it", or "at your discretion" in those verses.

Instead of opting for the most comfortable way to navigate this Christian life, let us be challenged by the way Jesus walked. Yes, His was a demonstration of power and dominion, but it also was a walk of obedience, of love, of faithfulness to His Father. If we are open to the Holy Spirit, the conviction will grow in us that we can do better than we have up to now — that there are actions we can take in order to please the Father more fully.

Any time we are aware of poor attitudes in us, we must recognize that the Spirit of God is dealing with us. He is showing us something about ourselves. We are not gaining that knowledge because of our high IQ. It is God who is showing us our present state and impressing on us the need to come up higher in Him.

God is not shining His light on us for the purpose of showing us what miserable wretches we are and how much we have missed it. He is yearning for us to walk like He does, talk like He does, act like He does. After all, He placed that divine seed in us, and why should He not receive a good harvest?!

> So God created man in His own image,
> in the image of God He created him; male
> and female He created them.
> Genesis 1:27

I believe God's faith says He can have a hundredfold return, don't you? His faith is extended on our behalf. He is just so good! Think of it: First He gives us the seed — faith — so that we can produce a harvest, and then He rewards us for bringing in the harvest!

Obedience is Better Than Sacrifice

Let's read what happened to the children of Israel after God had miraculously delivered them out of Egypt, their place of bondage:

> ...While it is said: *"Today, if you will hear His voice, Do not harden your hearts as in the rebellion."*
> For who, having heard, rebelled? Indeed, was it not all who came out of Egypt, led by Moses?
> Now with whom was He angry forty years? Was it not with those who sinned, whose corpses fell in the wilderness?
> And to whom did He swear that they would not enter His rest, but to those who did not obey?
> So we see that they could not enter in because of unbelief.
> Hebrews 3:15-19

As we read these verses, it may be hard to understand how the children of Israel could *not* have taken God at His Word, seeing they had encountered a miraculous deliverance out of the place of slavery. They knew from experience that God was true to His Word. He promised them deliverance and freedom, and that is what they received. He brought material prosperity to them in the form of jewels, gold and clothing which they were told to gather from their oppressors before leaving. They did not have a problem obeying God when it came to their financial prosperity. They did as they were told. They did not have a problem obeying God when it came to physical prosperity and preservation (note their complete obedience regarding the Passover — they did not want to die!) They obeyed! (See Genesis 12).

But once delivered from slavery, they put their own ideas and feelings above the expressed will of God. Maybe they thought they needed a rest from pressing on with God?

Does that sound familiar to any of us? How many of us have warred with the help of the written Word through the most difficult, trying circumstances to finally experience marvelous breakthrough, only to recline now and say, "Whew, I am glad this is over!" Friends, right after a victory is not the time to relax. Can you imagine what would happen to an earthly army that picked up all of their battle gear and went home right after they had won a victory? It's true, they won. It's true, they did a good job. But think back with me to World War II. What would have happened in Germany if the Allied Forces had withdrawn right after Germany capitulated? What would have happened in Japan? It was wisdom that called for the victors (the Allied Forces) to occupy after this costly, heart-wrenching war so that they could have a hand in the formation of a free and prosperous society. Else they would have given ground to opportunistic, malevolent forces which would have preyed on the weak, defeated citizenry. So likewise we must remain diligent and alert after having come through a battle. We must secure the ground gained. We might have to enforce our victory again. The Lord says, "Occupy till I come" (see Luke 19:13 KJV).

> ...*right after a victory is not the time to relax.*

The Apostle Paul had these encouraging words to say:

> ... My son, be strong in the grace that is in Christ Jesus.
> ... Endure hardship as a good soldier of Jesus Christ.
> No one engaged in warfare entangles himself with the affairs of this life, that he may please him who enlisted him as a soldier.
> 2 Timothy 2:1; 3, 4

The children of Israel had experienced a miraculous deliverance. They had come through tremendous pressures with flying colors. They had passed a great test. Now God was revealing to them how to stay alive and prosper. He told them when to gather the manna, how much to gather, and when not to gather.

Alas, they followed their carnal inclinations. I am sure they had several good reasons for doing what *they* thought was best. But they did not obey God.

I believe God could have caused the manna to stay fresh for a week, if all He wanted them to do was to gather it once a week. In telling them to gather it every day, He was emphasizing their need of Him every new day. God doesn't just do things a certain way to be difficult or hard-nosed. He has His reasons, and furthermore, God is not obligated to explain His reasons to us. We are to simply trust and obey Him regardless of what we think and how we feel about it, because He is God! He always has our best interests in mind.

The Word of God says,

> For My thoughts are not your thoughts,
> nor are your ways My ways, says the Lord.
> For as the heavens are higher than the earth,
> So are My ways higher than your ways,
> and My thoughts than your thoughts.
>
> Isaiah 55:8, 9

Let's not argue with God. He is smarter than we are! He is God! God was training the children of Israel to obey Him. They needed to know that obedience to God would entail His continued blessings. He was getting ready to lead them into territory that was occupied by enemies. He had to know that they would follow His instructions, or their destruction by these enemies was inevitable. He knew what they were up against. They didn't!

As we read later, they did not obey Him but did as they thought best. If the Lord had allowed that disobedient generation to enter the land He had promised them, Israel would not have been able to stand against her enemies, and God's plan—to have a people of His own in a land they would possess as their inheritance—would have been foiled. As it turned out, His plan was delayed 40 years. We see the wisdom of our God as He patiently waited for the next generation to set their collective hearts on Him.

Prayer: Father, please forgive me when I have been stubborn, insisting on my own way, leaning on my own understanding. I need Your help, Lord; I want to do better! You are my good, good Father. I am

Your beloved child. Teach me how to abide in You at all times so when the pressures of life come and I want to take things into my own hands, I will instead yield to Your leading, knowing that You have my best interests at heart. Amen.

Fellowship and Forgiveness

As children of God we know the necessity and the value of fellowshipping with our Father God. There really is no growing up in Him unless we spend time with Him, get to know Him, find out what He thinks about certain issues, and do that on a regular, daily basis.

We find ourselves in challenging circumstances sometimes, and sadly we do not respond in a way that reflects the character of God. When we know that we have missed the mark, we go to our Father God and acknowledge that we have fallen short, we call it by the name that He calls it, and we ask His forgiveness. According to His Word, He is faithful and just to forgive us our sins, and to cleanse us from all unrighteousness (1 John 1:7-9).

It would be great if that were all He required of us, but so often forgiveness needs a corresponding action. God may require us to humbly make amends with the offended or injured party. If we determine to learn from this, it will result in greater watchfulness and sensitivity to Holy Spirit. So we do whatever He requires of us, and we don't murmur or complain, even if it feels like it's costing a pound of our flesh.

Sometimes we find ourselves in a really bad situation that we did not initiate. Nevertheless, in that particular situation we responded in a way which did not please God, and we know it. So let's name the portion of the situation that we take ownership of, and let's not wait for the other party to initiate reconciliation. They may never admit to any wrongdoing. However, we are "in the clear" with God now because we owned up to the part we played in the situation. We can go on with our life without stumbling stones and rocks of offense littering our path. We can pursue our destiny in God.

I am convinced that the laissez-faire attitude of some Christians in regard to forgiveness is a major reason for the lack of spiritual growth. We cannot treat God like a senior citizen in a retirement home, who we think should be grateful for every visitor who stops by to affirm his love, devotion, and occasional regret for staying away too long. No! God is a holy God! He is a just God! Hebrews 2:2 says, "... *every transgression and disobedience received a just reward....*"

God has not changed. We are so quick to point out that He is the same yesterday, today, and forever when we need something that we see He provided in the past, and we even remind Him that He is no respecter of persons.

> *...to walk in the blessings of God, we must live in obedience to the instructions He laid out in His Word.*

But let us rightly divide the Word of God. The only unconditional facet of God is His love. He loves us regardless of who we are or what we've done. But have you noticed that to walk in the blessings of God, we must live in obedience to the instructions

He laid out in His Word? God does not bless disobedience. He does not change His Word because of our ignorance.

God wanted more than anything for the children of Israel to come into their inheritance, and though He was poised and ready to defend them, and to make up in wisdom and strength where they were lacking in order to subdue their enemies, He could not violate His own Word.

In Hebrews 3 it says that disobedience is the same as "an evil heart of unbelief." We must come to a deeper understanding of the fact that God hates sin, regardless of who commits it. His balances are just. He does not have one set of weights for the saint and another for the sinner. Sin is sin. As long as we entertain evil in our hearts, the Lord will not hear us (Psalm 66:18)!

We may be on our knees all day and all night, reminding the Lord of His Word concerning healing, expecting Him to perform His Word. But if we have ignored His nudge to forgive a certain person, or to make matters right where we have wronged someone, for instance, we are just wasting our breath in praying against that mountain of sickness, because we are not obeying Him. We are not forgiving, and neither can we be forgiven.

There is much suffering today because of disobedience to the cardinal law of God:

> . . . You shall love the Lord your God with all your heart, with all your soul, with all your strength, and with all your mind, and your neighbor as yourself.
> Luke 10:27

Children suffer today because of the disobedience of their parents. Wives or husbands suffer because of the disobedience of their spouse. Sin will not only try to destroy you, but your entire household will be affected by it. We cannot "compartmentalize" ungodly activities and think that because they are hidden, no one will be harmed or affected by it, be it our own body, our family, church or work.

God is not out to rob us of the "good times"; He wants to do us good all the days of our lives! He wants to bless us, but we must desire Him. We must want His presence and welcome His correction.

Some people wonder why they don't get their prayers answered and actually are half-mad at God, the preacher, the Bible, or all three. Someone remarked just recently in a very casual way (yet his desperation was evident to me) that he was convinced his communication line to God had a scrambling device attached to it, preventing his prayers from being heard on high.

We know for certain that God is on our side, and we need to act like it. Never blame God, but examine yourself to see if you are full of faith *and* faithful to Him. For a long time, I have had a big note on my bathroom mirror, reminding me that *without faith it is impossible to please God* (Hebrews 11:6), followed by *". . . and faith works by love"* (1 Corinthians 13), enumerating all the qualities of divine love. That *is* the challenge of the ages, and we must rise to it. (Hint: It's called laying down our lives to take up His.)

Prayer: Lord, when I think that it's too hard to forgive a person for what they've done, remind me of the day You found me and redeemed me out of darkness into Your marvelous light. Remind me of the insurmountable debt You paid so I could be free from every bondage and every snare. Let Your compassion rise up in me for the person who has wronged me, and give me Your words to speak over them — words of life and victory. Amen.

Developing our Trust in God

"Blessed be the God and Father of our Lord Jesus Christ, who has blessed us with every spiritual blessing in the heavenly places in Christ" (Ephesians 1:3).

God is trustworthy! Yet, we must obey Him and live uprightly. We must believe and act like we are the righteousness of God in Him, and follow after Him with all our hearts, to enjoy His blessings.

God admonished the Israelites to tell their children and children's children of His mighty acts, not because He was on an ego trip. No. He wanted the generations to know and not forget, and hear in their own ears again and again, that He was their Almighty God, their Deliverer, their Provider, their Healer, their Peace, their Righteousness, their All-Sufficiency, their Victory. He wants today's generations to know that He is on their side; He is for them and not against them; that they can count on Him to see them victoriously through any challenge *if* they will walk in His ways.

Our Lord Jesus gave this very simple, yet profound illustration of two kinds of people — the wise and the foolish. (I think those are the only two kinds there are!)

> Therefore whoever hears these sayings of Mine, and does them, I will liken him to a wise man who built his house on the rock:
> and the rain descended, the floods came, and the winds blew and beat on that house; and it did not fall, for it was founded on the rock.
> But everyone who hears these sayings of Mine, and does not do them, will be like a foolish man who built his house on the sand:
> and the rain descended, the floods came, and the winds blew and beat on that house; and it fell. And great was its fall.
>
> Matthew 7:24-27

We can count on this: The storms of life will come to everyone in one form or another. No one is immune from them. So what was it that determined preservation for one and destruction for the other? It was obedience! One man heard the Word of God and did it—he honored and showed respect to the Lord. The Lord in turn honored the man, and what this man had built was kept safe. The other man heard the same Word of God but did not apply it to his life, and what he had built was swept away. He gave God nothing to work with; there was nothing to honor.

Jesus did not mince words. He went right to the heart of the matter. He said that whoever *heard and did* His sayings would stand. We must be doers of the Word of God, and not hearers only!

On a recent visit overseas I was told the true story of a father and his son who went helicopter-skiing high in the mountains.

As these two were making their way down a slope, the father saw an avalanche forming. He yelled to his son, "Turn right!" and the son instantly obeyed. It made the difference between life and death. The avalanche roared past them. Both of them are alive to talk about it—with a good deal of emotion—the son with gratitude to the father for saving his life, and the father glad beyond measure that his son listened to him, thus allowing him to save his life.

Now, if the son had been like some of us, he might have asked for three good reasons why he should make a right turn . . . why not a left turn, or maybe even go straight? What was wrong with maintaining the same direction he was headed in? Well, fundamentally there is nothing wrong with turning right, left, or going straight. But in this particular instance it was not the time to keep on doing what he had been doing—it was critical that he changed direction!

What a vivid illustration of everyday life this was to me to portray a Bible truth. We must come to the place in Him where He has the absolute right-of-way in our lives, in every situation. Instant obedience to His voice will, in many cases, make the difference between preservation and destruction.

We are entering a place in time where we will have to be so in tune with Father God that indeed "in Him we

> *Instant obedience to His voice will, in many cases, make the difference between preservation and destruction.*

live, and move, and have our being," and the Lord can say the same thing about Himself: "In him or in her I live, and move, and have My being." This may sound farfetched, but isn't that what Jesus was praying to the Father?

> ... That they all may be one, as You, Father, are in Me, and I in You; that they also may be one in Us, that the world may believe that You sent Me.
> And the glory which You gave Me I have given them, that they may be one just as We are one:
> I in them, and You in Me, that they may be made perfect in one, and that the world may know that You have sent Me, and have loved them as You have loved Me.
>
> John 17:21-23

Is He living and moving in us to the full expression of His nature? Have we done away with our own ideas and ways so that He can truly be God in us? He longs to reveal Himself through us in glorious ways as the Almighty, the Deliverer, the Defender, the Healer ... not just for our benefit but also as a sign and a wonder to those who are still outside the family of God who, when they see His great goodness demonstrated before their very eyes, will turn to Him to be made whole — spirit, soul and body.

Prayer: Lord, You are trustworthy...You are faithful! There is no good reason to doubt Your trustworthiness or faithfulness. Help me to trust You more and more each day. Amen.

Recognizing our Place

We need to recognize and accept the place that we have been called to in God's plan for this time. At the heart of everything that the Lord ever did was redemption. He never wanted His creation to be lost, in darkness, and eternally separated from Him. God desires to show Himself strong to His people in every aspect of this life. The people of God are to so reflect the goodness and mercy and loveliness of God that those outside His family will be drawn to Him, compelled to make a decision. It is the goodness of God lived out through us, His family, that will bring them in. If we allow God to have His way in us, nothing will be impossible, and we will truly be an honor, a glory, and a praise to Him.

> *If we allow God to have His way in us, nothing will be impossible....*

In Genesis 11:5, 6 we read:

> But the Lord came down to see the city and the tower which the sons of men had built.
> And the Lord said, "Indeed the people are one and they all have one language, and this is what they begin to do; now nothing that they propose to do will be withheld from them."

The Lord Himself said that because the people were as one—they were in one accord—nothing would be impossible that they had conceived in their minds. Let's turn this around to the positive side. If we will become one with God, meaning we are of one heart and one mind with Him, nothing will be impossible—nothing will be withheld from us—that we can conceive by His Spirit!

The Bible says that *"he who is joined to the Lord is one spirit with Him"* (1 Corinthians 6:17). When we realize this truth fully, we will live like Him, act like Him, talk like Him, look just like Him. . . we will be full of His glorious presence. We will feel what He feels, desire what He desires, and we will also have real dislikes, the same dislikes He has.

We have seen the glory and the power of God manifested in different places. God intends to produce in us more than just goosebumps and a story to tell the next day. He *is* the glory. He *is* the power.

Prayer: Lord, I want to be in the place that You have called me to at this time. Help me to recognize Your leading. Put people in my path to help me. Give me the grace to make all necessary adjustments with a joyful heart. Help me appreciate the fact that every member of the family of God is important to our success. Amen.

Total Commitment

Holy Spirit has been stirring our hearts to seek Him more and more. The challenge has been put in front of us. We are recognizing that a dividing line is being drawn, and those of us sitting on the fence will have to get off. No longer are we a people who sit around idly, content with where we are. God has always had an army, but He is gearing up for the greatest display of His power that this world has ever known, and we need to get ready. We need to get into battle array. But before we can proceed with that, let's make sure that we don't carry any extra weights with us that would only hinder us and slow us down.

If we will desire the presence of God, we will be changed. His presence will transform us—it will conform us to the image that He desires. His light and His glory will expose our liabilities—the ones we know about and may have been dealing with repeatedly, and also the ones we are not aware of—the ones that are on our blind side, so to speak.

Several years ago during praise and worship at church, the Lord gave me a vision. It seemed that I was walking back and forth in front of very ornate, high wrought iron gates, trying to figure out how to open them, as I was intrigued with the beautiful, immaculately kept garden that lay beyond. Whatever I tried to get them to open, they did not move. But as we were praising and worshipping the Lord, all of a sudden these enormous gates opened slowly, and in my heart I knew that it was the thanksgiving and praise which caused the gates to swing open. It was then that I had the liberty to enter.

The garden was enormous in size and reached as far as the eye could see, reminding me of the formal, stately gardens I had seen in Europe. Every fifty yards or so stood a beautiful fountain dispensing crystal clear water. Impulsively I dipped my hands, then my arms up to my elbows, and when I could not get satisfied just splashing this water on me which felt so wonderful and was so refreshing, I threw myself into the shallow water of that fountain. I began to look for some deep water where I could get totally wet. Immediately I came upon a pool, and without the slightest hesitation I dove in and coursed effortlessly through the water. I was just as much "at home" under the water as I was on the surface. I did not seem to be in need of any air while I was immersed.

Eventually I got out. As I continued my walk, I came to a huge place that was lined with tall Greek columns on one side. Strolling through them, I reached a ledge. I leaned over the top, curious what lay beneath, and saw through a grey haze the earth spread out like a topographical map. I saw valleys and mountains, rivers and towns. I could not detect any movement—it all lay there so still.

As I was taking in this scene, I got the urge to fly. Thinking on that, I immediately found myself cruising through the air, as effortlessly as I had coursed the deep water not long before. What joy I experienced!

Soon the realization came to me that the reason I could fly was because I had absolutely no weights on me. I was free from anything that could have held me down.

The illumination I received through this vision changed my life. Most important, I saw that as I willingly and cheerfully submitted to the cleansing water (the Word of God), the power of God would be evident to such a degree that some natural laws would be superseded at a certain point in order to accomplish the will of God for that time.

Prayer: Lord, You are my Good Shepherd. Lead me to the cleansing streams, the still, clear waters in Your green pastures. Restore my soul and lead me on Your righteous path. Open my eyes to what You have prepared for me. Pour Your fresh oil on me until it overflows, changing the atmosphere around me. Amen.

Life-Giving Water

In Ezekiel 47 we read of healing waters—waters that reach to the ankles, then to the knees, then to the loins, and finally, they are deep enough to swim in. Having received a down payment of the Spirit of God at the New Birth is wonderful. We have indeed come to the flowing, living waters. But it is only the beginning of walking in this new dimension.

Let's see if we can find ourselves in the following illustration: A group of people finally arrive at the ocean, the aim of their journey. All are looking forward to the refreshing, cool water. Some are content to just play on the beach, knowing they are close to the water; that they can cool off by wading in the shallow part for a few minutes if they get hot. The water refreshes them. Aside from that, they don't have much use for it. They are the ones who go in ankle deep. They are very much in control of their own lives. Holy Spirit (the water) occasionally gets to minister to them, but they decide when and how.

Then there are those who will get into the water up to their knees. They can sense the awesome power of the ocean at this stage already because the wave action affects the balance of their entire body. Holy Spirit begins to point out to them areas in their lives that are not harmonious with the will and the nature of God.

By the time the waves reach people's loins, it may get downright uncomfortable, and at that point they decide to either go for a swim or get out of the water. It is powerful.

Not only can you swim in deep water, but have you ever played "dead man" in it? When I was a child, it was one of the fun things to do in water, especially after your arms and legs had gotten tired from swimming. You would "lay down" on top of the water, make your whole body stiff as a board, tilt the head back slightly, and not move. Effortlessly you could float like this as long as you "played dead." The moment you "resurrected"—made any kind of movement—you began to sink. You either had to start swimming to stay afloat, or you had to roll over and play dead again.

God desires for us to stay out in the deep waters every single day, for that is where He can accomplish the most through us. Let's decide today to get self-effort out of the way and allow Him to have His way in us.

Prayer: Lord, I confess that I tend to take charge so I can control outcomes. It is a challenge for me to give up control. Yet I know in my inward being that You are infinitely wiser, that You are the only One Who knows the beginning and the end of a matter, and You have already shown Your benevolent intent toward me by adopting me and giving me a place in Your family. I take You at Your word, Lord, that You will never leave me nor forsake me, and so I yield to Your promptings, to Your nudges, to the plans and purposes You have for me to cooperate with. Thank You, Lord, for being a present help at all times. Amen.

CHAPTER 4

TAKING THE HIGH ROAD: GOD'S RIGHTEOUS STANDARD

It is safe to assume that every one of us has been in situations that have given us the opportunity to judge, and we gladly obliged. Chances are that not many of us applied the standard of God, thereby in effect passing judgment on ourselves.

> But with righteousness He shall judge the poor, and decide with equity for the meek of the earth.
> Isaiah 11:4a

Here we have the expressed will of God concerning the standard that is to be applied in judgment: His righteousness.

> Judge not, that you be not judged.
> For with what judgment you judge, you will be judged; and with the measure you use, it will be measured back to you.
> Therefore, whatever you want men to do to you, do also to them, for this is the Law and the Prophets.

> Enter by the narrow gate; for wide is the gate and broad is the way that leads to destruction, and there are many who go in by it.
> Because narrow is the gate and difficult is the way which leads to life, and there are few who find it.
>
> Matthew 7:1, 2; 12-14

That narrow way seems to be a lonely road most of the time, but this we can know for certain—it is the high life! It is the way Jesus travelled. It is far above that wide road where people seemingly walk shoulder to shoulder because there are so many of them. On that wide road we find man's approval, man's wisdom, man's ability. But on this narrow path, the one that Jesus walked, we find God's approval, God's wisdom, God's ability. It is a way illuminated by His light, love, provision and protection.

Have you ever been pushed around, misunderstood, abused and hurt by people? It is particularly painful when the person is a brother or sister in the Lord. I was going in circles, as it were, over "one of those" situations, when Holy Spirit reminded me that as one who reigned in life with Christ Jesus (Romans 5:17), I had a scepter—the scepter of righteousness—which is the scepter of the Kingdom of God. Holy Spirit prodded me to see myself pointing my scepter at the person who had wronged me and pronouncing that individual *righteous*.

I consider myself to have by nature an acute sense of fairness, and this just did not seem fair to me! Here I was, the maligned one, and I was supposed to pronounce a blessing on a person and declare him or her righteous? *God, You can't mean that,* I thought. *Didn't you see what happened?* I wish I could say that I instantly obeyed, but that was not the case. It took many tears as I struggled with my "old nature" before I was willing to be obedient, to trust that God knew better.

However, concerning that particular situation, it was the first step to liberty for me. The gesture that I repeated in my mind whenever my feelings wanted to run away with me put me back on track every time. God allowed me to see a different perspective of the situation, and healing and liberty came.

All of us can do this with our brothers and sisters in Christ. I wish we never trespassed against each other, because we are not just hurting each other—we are the Body of Christ and therefore we are hurting Jesus. Surely He feels what we feel. The Bible says He is touched with the feelings of our infirmities and was in all things tempted like we are, yet without sin (Hebrews 4:15). Let us ask Him to show us how to deal with each situation.

Of course, in dealing with those not yet part of God's family we know to just forgive them and ask the Lord to forgive them as well, because they literally don't know what they are doing. They are walking in darkness, without God and without hope in the world. But we are called the children of light, and we have all it takes to properly represent our God, the King of the universe. There is no getting away from this—do we really, *really* believe that this Bible we call the Word of God is indeed His Word?

> ... His divine power has given to us all things that pertain to life and godliness, through the knowledge of Him who called us by glory and virtue,
> by which have been given to us exceedingly great and precious promises, that through these you may be partakers of the divine nature, having escaped the corruption that is in the world through lust.
>
> 2 Peter 1:3, 4

Unless we use the standard of God, which is His righteousness, we will not do justly. In fact, we will not be capable of doing justly. It takes knowledge of His Word — knowledge of Him, for He is the Word — to judge righteously. God and His Word are One. *God's Word is God speaking to us!* There is an urgent need for us today to get back to the standard of God, to see things the way He sees them, to recognize things for what they are, and to call those things by their proper name — the name God calls them.

Prayer: God, You know me better than I know myself. Wash over me with Your goodness and mercy and truth proceeding from Your heart of love. Teach me how to do the same for others. Amen.

When Light Comes

In the Old Testament we have the account of a man of God (he happened to be a prophet) who submitted himself to the righteous standard.

> In the year that King Uzziah died, I saw the Lord sitting on a throne, high and lifted up, and the train of His robe filled the temple.
> So I said, "Woe is me, for I am undone! Because I am a man of unclean lips, And I dwell in the midst of a people of unclean lips; For my eyes have seen the King, The Lord of hosts."
> Then one of the seraphim flew to me, having in his hand a live coal which he had taken with the tongs from the altar.
> And he touched my mouth with it, and said: "Behold, this has touched your lips, Your iniquity is taken away, And your sin purged."
> Also I heard the voice of the Lord, saying: "Whom shall I send, and who will go for Us?" Then I said, "Here am I! Send me."
> And He said, "Go...."
>
> Isaiah 6:1; 5–9a

Notice that it was when Isaiah *saw the Lord* that he recognized he was unclean. He saw himself in the true light. If Isaiah had looked to people around him and what they were doing, he would not have judged himself unclean. They were just as unclean as he was. Their "standard," if you will, was a reflection of his own condition.

As long as the world's people are our standard and we look to them and compare ourselves with them—even pattern ourselves after them—we will not advance in the Lord. What kind of illumination, what kind of counsel could we possibly receive from someone who is not walking in the Light and most likely in need of counsel and illumination himself?

It takes an encounter with God to reveal our condition. He will not force Himself on anyone—He is received. If we will make ourselves available to Him, He will reveal truth to us, and if we will receive it, it will set us free. When we come into His light, we will grow!

This reminds me of an interesting experiment I saw at a school science fair many years ago. A student wanted to emphasize the importance that light plays in developing plants to their full potential. Not only did the plants require light, it had to be the right kind of light. To illustrate this point, he raised several specimens, subjecting each to a different light. One plant received only blue light, while another received only red light, and yet another yellow light. The plant that received white light—which is "full spectrum" and includes all of the colors—was the only plant which truly thrived. The others existed the best they could with the particular light they got. They were yellowish, spindly-looking, frail little plants, not at all attractive to behold.

How do people outside the Kingdom of God perceive us? Are we to be desired because we are thriving and wholesome, or are we yellowish, sick little Christians? We all know the answer. Family of God, this must not be so any longer! Let us get into the light of God's Word so we will thrive.

Prayer: Father, You desire for me to prosper in every way, and You have let me know that Your light, Your illumination, will accomplish this. Today I ask You to shine Your light on those areas in me that need Your life-giving light. I receive it gladly! I praise You that I am on my way to being perfect and entire, lacking no good thing. Amen.

What Does God Require of Us?

God has this to say in His Word:

> As obedient children, not conforming yourselves to the former lusts, as in your ignorance; but as He who called you is holy, you also be holy in all your conduct,
> because it is written, "Be holy, for I am holy."
> 1 Peter 1:14–16

We know that God is fair, and He is just. He will not command us to do or be something that is impossible for us to do or be. If God says for us to be holy, we can be holy! The following verses will show us how this is possible.

> ...You were not redeemed with corruptible things, like silver and gold, from your aimless conduct received by tradition from your fathers,
> but with the precious blood of Christ, as of a lamb without blemish and without spot.
> He indeed was foreordained before the foundation of the world, but was manifest in these last times for you
> who through Him believe in God, who raised Him from the dead and gave Him glory, so that your faith and hope are in God.
> 1 Peter 1:18–21

We see from the preceding verses that we are precious to God; we are holy to Him because we were redeemed with the precious and holy blood of the Lord Jesus Christ. God is righteous, and He has given us His righteousness so we can live righteously. God is holy, and He has given us His holiness so we can live holy lives before Him.

We may look at the Scriptures and see that they command us to be holy, but we wonder how in the world we can possibly do that. Brothers and sisters, holiness is not a dress code. It is not a certain mannerism of speech. As a matter of fact, being holy is not any outward thing that we could do or say. Holiness takes place on the inside of us—in our hearts—and then finds expression outwardly.

Holiness takes place on the inside of us...and then finds expression outwardly.

The divine substance of our human spirit that came alive when we received Jesus as our Savior is the same substance that will enable us to walk in holiness: faith.

It takes faith, for instance, to walk in God's love. We have to receive that truth into our hearts, and when we do, our actions will speak of what we believe. Whatever we have in abundance in our hearts will find expression through our actions. James 2:14 says, *"What good is it, brethren, if a man has faith and no corresponding actions?"* (WNT). Faith demands expression.

It is God's will for us to walk holy before Him. We have to make the decision to receive that Word and then walk it out in our daily life. Whatever we are willing to believe of the Word of God will benefit us. If we believe God wants us well, for instance, divine healing can be a reality in our lives. If we believe that one tenth of our income belongs to the Lord and we honor Him with our tithes and offerings, God blesses the rest—prosperity finds us.

Conversely, if we do not believe that we can live a holy life, chances are we are living a mediocre Christian existence, and we are miserable!

But we know from the previous Scriptures that the Lord expects us to be holy, and He calls it "our reasonable service."

> I beseech you therefore, brethren, by the mercies of God, that you present your bodies a living sacrifice, holy, acceptable to God, *which is your reasonable service.*
> And do not be conformed to this world, but be transformed by the renewing of your mind, that you may prove what is that good and acceptable and perfect will of God.
>
> Romans 12:1, 2

We can see that there is a process involved. We are to renew our minds to the ways of God and then we can prove what the good, acceptable, and perfect will of God is. It's not the other way around. A renewed mind and heart in tune with God's heart is equipped to represent Him well.

A renewed mind and heart in tune with God's heart is equipped to represent Him well.

Notice, too, that God calls for a living sacrifice, not just one that "dedicates" him or herself once and then waits for the Rapture. No, He wants men and women, boys and girls dedicated to Him spirit, soul and body, a people He can work through. He wants a people who will listen to His voice and do His will, who will forget preconceived ideas and past notions and just go with Him!

Some may take issue with "hearing the voice of God." Is Jesus Christ our Good Shepherd? If we are His sheep, He expects us to hear His voice! He says, "My sheep hear My voice, and I know them, and they follow Me" (John 10:27).

Whatever anyone ever did for God was done one step at a time. There is not a single person who knows each individual step that needs to be taken right up to the time they go home to be with Jesus. No, we walk with God one step at a time, one minute at a time, one hour at a time, one day at a time.

That is a very comforting thought to me. It takes all the worry and anxiety away about missing God. I am responsible to live holy before God this minute, to reflect Him this minute, to represent Him this minute. I don't have to worry about ten days from now. Instead, this minute I draw near to God. I let Him live His life through me. And then I do it the next minute, and the next, and so on.

> *If we love God in deed and not in word only... we will be doers of His Word, not hearers and "quoters" only.*

Jesus is saying to us today, "If you love Me, keep My commandments." That is the bottom line. If we love God in deed and not in word only, we will keep His commandments; we will be doers of His Word, not hearers and "quoters" only.

The things we permit in our lives will rule us to one degree or another. God admonishes us today to choose life, which is His divine life, *zoe*, the God-kind of life. And why wouldn't we? If we should still think we've got a better, easier, or more amiable way figured out, we have not submitted to His kingship. Let's be teachable, allow Holy Spirit to train us, and esteem the precious truths revealed to us in the Word as priceless treasures indeed.

As we study the Word of God, let's apply it to our lives and make it our daily bread. Whatever parts of our lives we choose to leave the Word of God out of, whatever parts are not included in our daily bread, are not receiving any nourishment. They are bound for failure, are dying, or are already dead.

We need to see things as they truly are. Is there any area in our life that is a whitewashed tomb—a private place for dead people? Then that part of us "stinketh" because of decay, and after a while it will affect other parts. If the Lord reveals such an area, allow the light of God's Word to impart new life. Things brought out in the open and repented of will lose their power over you.

Prayer: Lord, it's me again! I want to thank You that You have redeemed me, and You continue to redeem every part of me that I offer up to You. It is a fact that, because I submit to You, I am becoming more whole each time I go through this process with You — it is a process! I am becoming more like You. Thank You, Lord! Amen.

Divine Digestion

By now we have recognized the need to give the Word of God first place in our lives. We know the way to prevail is to have an attitude of "come rain or shine, popular or not, this is what God says, I believe it, and that settles it."

However, in our zeal for God, let us also walk in the wisdom of God. One of the reasons there seems to be some confusion and disappointment in the Body of Christ concerning certain issues is that some of us are running around with truths and revelations that have not been afforded the necessary meditation in our hearts, that have not been rightly divided, that have been only halfway digested, so to speak.

Not that they aren't revelations by the Spirit of God, not that they aren't true — they are. But just as the physical body absorbs and takes into the system natural food, and requires a certain amount of time to assimilate it, our spirit man — the inner man, the real you, the part that is alive eternally — has to be given time and opportunity to assimilate spiritual food.

The Apostle Paul had this to say to the Church at Philippi: "Therefore, my beloved, as you have always obeyed, not as in my presence only, but now much more in my absence, work out your own salvation with fear and trembling; for it is God who works in you both to will and to do for His good pleasure" (Philippians 2:12,13).

The Dangerous Place of Presumption

We need to develop a sense of stewardship over the riches of God's Word. His Word is alive! It is full of power! It is dynamite! But how many realize that we have to know how to use the dynamite; how to plant it in certain strategic locations, in order for it to be most effective? We don't just run around and throw some here, there, and everywhere. No, we have more sense than that—we want to live!

There was a certain understanding in the Church which led to a flippant attitude toward the Word of God. It was as if we were putting God over a barrel, saying, "God, Your Word states . . . ." We learned every Scripture reference to every blessing God ever promised. We knew that God didn't lie, and that He had exalted His Word above His Name, so we believed we were in a place where God had to perform His Word. We "worked the Word" like a formula, with the expectation that the Word had to work if we pulled the right levers and pushed the right buttons. Friend, the Word is a Person! He is not a slot machine! A place of assuming and presuming is a dangerous place to be. Everything concerning God proceeds out of covenant, relationship and Fatherhood.

Out of our deep fellowship with God will we receive every promise He has secured through the blood of His Son.

Too many times we sink, trying to "walk on the water." The Spirit and the Word have to agree, family! If what we are believing God for proceeds out of a heart of covenant devotion to God, which is the heart of God, we will have good success. But if our motives are self-serving, we should be prepared for a few swimming lessons.

God does not have to prove anything to us. He did it once and for all at the Cross of Calvary!

Let us become sensitive to Holy Spirit. Let us become sensitive to the Word of God.

First Peter 4:10, 11 says this:

> As each one has received a gift, minister it to one another, as good stewards of the manifold grace of God.
> If anyone speaks, let him speak as the oracles of God. If anyone ministers, let him do it as with the ability which God supplies, that in all things God may be glorified through Jesus Christ, to whom belong the glory and the dominion forever and ever. Amen.

The Apostle Paul exhorts the Church to *"receive not the grace of God in vain…we give no offense in anything, that our ministry may not be blamed"* (2 Corinthians 6:1; 3). We must live the things that we preach! Just read on in verses 4–10 and see how Paul lived. It's an eye opener.

Let us not be as those people Paul referred to in his letter to Timothy who have "a form of godliness but denying its power" (see 2 Timothy 3:5). The Holy Spirit, the Teacher of the Church, desires to establish us in our faith, to teach us line upon line. Let's give Him our time and energy so we can grow up in all things.

Prayer: Father, my heart cries out to You like David's in Psalm 25:4, 5, who said, "Show me Your ways, O Lord; Teach me Your paths. Lead me in Your truth and teach me, For You are the God of my salvation; On You I wait all the day." Amen.

Walking in Newness of Life

In reading through the Bible, and especially the New Testament, we come to recognize how practical God is. God's Word provides detailed instructions on what to do and what not to do. Our Father does not leave us guessing as to what He likes and what He doesn't like. We don't have any excuses for not doing what pleases God!

For the sake of putting all of us in remembrance, let us look at the following Scriptures.

> If then you were raised with Christ, seek those things which are above, where Christ is, sitting at the right hand of God.
> Set your mind on things above, not on things on the earth.
> For you died, and your life is hidden with Christ in God.
> Colossians 3:1-3

In verses 1 and 2 we are told to seek those things that are above and to set our affection on them, not on earthly things. Our aim is not just to miss Hell and go to Heaven, and in the meantime live any way we want to. No!

We were redeemed with the precious blood of Christ! God hates sin! We get a picture of how much God hates sin by the offering that was required to atone for sin and to enable us to live above it.

Think about the price that was paid! Meditate on what Jesus went through for you so that you would not have to be dominated by sin.

Verse 3 says we are dead, meaning our old nature—that sinful nature—died on Calvary together with Christ. Why is the Spirit of God so adamant about us, the Body of Christ, identifying with the death of Jesus that He repeats it in several other places? He wants to get a point across to us. Just as you repeat words to someone if you want to be sure that you were heard, Holy Spirit is repeating Himself in various other places in Scripture.

> How should we respond to all of this? Is it good to persist in a life of sin so that grace may multiply even more?

Absolutely not! How can we die to a life where sin ruled over us and then invite sin back into our lives?

Did someone forget to tell you that when we were initiated into Jesus the Anointed through baptism's ceremonial washing, we entered into His death?

Therefore, we were buried with Him through this baptism into death so that just as God the Father, in all His glory, resurrected the Anointed One, we, too, might walk confidently out of the grave into a new life.

To put it another way: If we have been united with Him to share in a death like His, don't you understand that we will also share in His resurrection?

We know this: whatever we used to be with our old sinful ways has been nailed to His cross. So our entire record of sin has been canceled, and we no longer have to bow down to sin's power.

A dead man, you see, cannot be bound by sin. But if we have died with the Anointed One, we believe that we shall also live together with Him.

So we stand firm in the conviction that death holds no power over God's Anointed, because He was resurrected from the dead never to face death again.

When He died, He died to whatever power sin had, once and for all, and now He lives completely to God.

So here is how to picture yourself now that you have been initiated into Jesus the Anointed: you are dead to sin's power and influence, but you are alive to God's rule.

Don't invite that insufferable tyrant of sin back into your mortal body so you won't become obedient to its destructive desires.

Don't offer your bodily members to sin's service as tools of wickedness; instead, offer your body to God as those who are alive from the dead, and devote the parts of your body to God as tools for justice and goodness in this world.

For sin is no longer a tyrant over you; indeed you are under grace and not the law.

So what do we do now? Throw ourselves into lives of sin because we are cloaked in grace and don't have to answer to the law? Absolutely not!

Doesn't it make sense that if you sign yourself over as a slave, you will have to obey your master? The question before you is, What will be your master?

Will it be sin—which will lead to certain death—or obedience—which will lead to a right and reconciled life?

Romans 6:1-16 (The Voice)

God tells us in verse 11 to reckon, to consider, to regard or think of ourselves as dead to sin's power. Not just dead, but dead *indeed!* Truly! Undeniably! In reality! As a matter of fact! *Indeed!*

Just as surely, as truly, as undeniably as we know that we will go to Heaven when we die because Hell has no claim, power or authority over us, we must know that we can live righteous, holy lives because sin (the old nature) has no claim, power or authority over us. We are called to walk in newness of life.

Prayer: Lord, You are my Master. You redeemed me from all destruction and set my feet on solid rock—Your Word. I stand surefooted on Your Word, and praise You that You are working mightily in me, conforming me to Your image. Amen.

A Revelation of Redemption

We need a revelation of what it means to be redeemed. Webster's definition of *redeem* means: a) to buy back, repurchase; to get or win back; b) to free from what distresses or harms: as, to free from captivity by payment of ransom, to extricate from or help to overcome something detrimental, to release from blame or debt: to clear, to free from consequences of sin; c) to change for the better: reform; d) repair, restore; e) to free from a lien by payment of an amount secured thereby, to remove the obligation of…by payment, to convert into something of value, to make good: fulfill; f) to atone for: expiate, to offset the bad effect of: to make worthwhile: retrieve.

This little word *redeemed* alone is shouting ground! Hallelujah! See yourself bought back, freed from all that distresses or harms, freed from captivity, released from blame or debt, cleared and free from the tentacles of sin.

If we would get an understanding of the truth that we were redeemed from sin as much as we were redeemed from eternal separation from God, we'd have far fewer struggles to go through. If ever an attempt were made to convince the believer that he had to go to Hell, it would be met with strenuous objection. "No," he'd say, "I know my Savior died for me and with His own blood paid the ransom for me; I stand on His blood and His righteousness, and I am going to Heaven!"

This same conviction of Heaven being our home ought to be the same that drives our lives here and now. God's Word says that "sin shall not have dominion over you" — shall not be a tyrant over you. Jesus is our Lord. Since He is our Lord, our

Master, our King, we must conduct ourselves in a manner that is befitting the Kingdom of God. We are called His ambassadors in Second Corinthians 5:20. Let us walk worthy of the Lord, pleasing Him in all that we think, say, and do.

Put on the New Man

The Word of God gives us practical instructions on how we live this out: We put on the new man referred to in Colossians 3 and elsewhere.

Notice, *we* put on the new man. Nobody else is going to do it for us, *we* put him on.

> Therefore put to death your members which are on the earth: fornication, uncleanness, passion, evil desire, and covetousness, which is idolatry.
> Because of these things the wrath of God is coming upon the sons of disobedience,
> in which you yourselves once walked when you lived in them.
> But now you yourselves are to put off all these: anger, wrath, malice, blasphemy, filthy language out of your mouth.
> Do not lie to one another, since you have put off the old man with his deeds,
> and have put on the new man who is renewed in knowledge according to the image of Him who created him,
> where there is neither Greek nor Jew, circumcised nor uncircumcised, barbarian, Scythian, slave nor free, but Christ is all and in all.
> Therefore, as the elect of God, holy and beloved, put on tender mercies, kindness, humility, meekness, longsuffering;
> bearing with one another, and forgiving

one another, if anyone has a complaint against another; even as Christ forgave you, so you also must do.

But above all these things put on love, which is the bond of perfection.

And let the peace of God rule in your hearts, to which also you were called in one body; and be thankful.

Let the word of Christ dwell in you richly in all wisdom, teaching and admonishing one another in psalms and hymns and spiritual songs, singing with grace in your hearts to the Lord.

And whatever you do in word or deed, do all in the name of the Lord Jesus, giving thanks to God the Father through Him.

And whatever you do, do it heartily, as to the Lord and not to men,

knowing that from the Lord you will receive the reward of the inheritance; for you serve the Lord Christ.

Colossians 3:5–17; 23, 24

We clearly see that whatever good and profitable thing God wants to work through us is dependent on our obedience to Him. He desires to be God in us! He longs to manifest Himself through us!

Notice, though, the little word "if" in the following Scripture:

This is a faithful saying: For if we died with Him, we shall also live with Him.

If we endure, we shall also reign with Him. If we deny Him, He also will deny us.

If we are faithless, He remains faithful; He cannot deny Himself.

2 Timothy 2:11–13

God cannot deny Himself. He is holy, and pure, and just. He cannot be God in and through us to the degree He desires as long as we choose our own ways and walk in our own human wisdom. Let us meditate and understand the words of Jesus who said, "... *he who loses his life for My sake will find it*" (Matthew 10:39b). The abundant life is walking in close fellowship with our Lord, seeing, listening, and understanding what His will is for us at this moment, and being willing and obedient to walk the path He has prepared for us.

Prayer: Father, help me to always be willing and obedient to what I know Your plans and purposes are for me. Amen.

A Word on Praise

The Book of James is a statement on ethical Christian living. As such, it does not debate or speculate on how we as believers should conduct ourselves but offers straightforward instructions for us.

Of particular interest for us here is verse 2 of the first chapter which reads, "*My brethren, count it all joy **when** you fall into various trials . . . .*" Notice that James did not say "*if* you fall into trials," so the implied truth is that trials will come to us all. In Chapter 4 verse 7 we read this admonition: "*. . . Submit to God. Resist the devil and he will flee from you.*"

Sounds good, doesn't it? But how exactly do we do this? Well, there are a number of ways. One that comes to mind right away is acting on the knowledge of our covenant rights, privileges, and duties. We always want to remember, it is not by our own wisdom or works or goodness that we come through victoriously, but it is by the provision, the leadership, the grace, the workings, and the presence of our God.

Several years ago I participated in a seminar on intercessory warfare through worship, and the Lord let me catch a glimpse of what happens in the spirit realm when we release praise and worship to Him. All of a sudden I saw this creature similar to a big old manatee. A manatee is related to the elephant but lives in the water, and here in Florida, where I live, manatee can be found all along the coast line. This creature that I saw was lying on dry land. Its thick, stiff skin was of a battleship grey color and had little jets or pipes protruding from it, about half an inch long, a great number of them. When worship from God's people would rise up to the heavens, the wind or breath of the worship would activate the little jets on the creature and the sound would blow through them, causing this creature to writhe in great torment and terror.

Immediately the Lord brought Ezekiel 28:13-16 to mind:

> You were in Eden, the garden of God; every precious stone was your covering. . . .
> The workmanship of your timbrels and pipes was prepared for you on the day you were created.
> You were the anointed cherub who covers; I established you; you were on the holy mountain of God; you walked back and forth in the midst of fiery stones.
> You were perfect in your ways from the day you were created, till iniquity was found in you . . . .
> . . .Therefore I cast you as a profane thing out of the mountain of God. . . .

Throughout my life I have read a number of books on praise and worship, and they were all good. However, after being shown this creature (which represents our adversary the devil, the enemy of everything good and God) in such a helpless and tormented state because of the worship being released, I got a new and deeper appreciation for the power that is released in praise and worship. The anointing—the presence of God—breaks every yoke!

Remember the One from whom all blessings flow, and also be aware who the destroyer is: *"The thief does not come except to steal, and to kill, and to destroy. I have come that they may have life, and that they may have it more abundantly"* (John 10:10).

I want to encourage you to use this weapon of worship in warfare so you gain new ground for yourself, your loved ones, and the Kingdom of God the next time you feel like your back is against the wall. Sing to the Lord with the voice of triumph. Make His praise glorious! Put your heart and soul into worshipping God and experience His presence in the way you need Him in that moment. I am convinced God is more determined for us to break free from oppression than we are many times.

Let us not receive His marvelous grace in vain, but let us fight the good fight of faith without flinching or letting up. Believe that the little pin prick of faith in the dam of adversity will spell defeat for the plans of the adversary, and trust God to bring it about.

CHAPTER 5

THIRTY-FIVE BLESSINGS OF FEARING THE LORD

We read in Hebrews 11:6 that it is impossible to please God without faith. A simple definition for Bible faith that comes to mind is believing what God says is true, and acting on it. We have people today who say they have faith, but their actions do not correspond with their words. We must place importance in our words—they are filled with power. Read the first and third chapters of James to appreciate the power of words more fully. I want you to know that your faith won't accomplish much if you are disobedient. The heroes of faith we read about in Hebrews 11 were men and women of obedience. Faith in God means obedience to God.

Faith in God means obedience to God.

Personal experience taught me that any time I disobey God knowingly, I have come to a standstill as far as my walk with Him is concerned. At the point where I become aware that I am not advancing, I need to ask the Lord to show me what the last thing was He required of me, and then obey Him and do it! I will not go any further until I obey Him.

Every Word of God is profitable for us, able to correct and instruct us in righteousness, the standard of God. Let's take a look at some of the outstanding examples of faith mentioned in the Bible.

In Genesis 6 through 8 we read the account of the flood which destroyed everyone on the face of the earth except the occupants in the ark. Noah obeyed God, and not only was his life spared, but he and his family became the progenitors of the human race after the deluge. The Lord said to Noah, "Come into the ark, you and all your household, because I have seen that you are righteous before Me in this generation" (Genesis 7:1). How could God say that? Because Noah believed God, and he obeyed Him. He feared the Lord! The reward of obedience was that Noah and his entire household were saved from destruction.

Genesis 12 through 18 tells us of Abraham's relationship with God. It was one of trust and obedience, prompting Abram to forsake his homeland and follow God. Genesis 15:6 says, *"And he believed in the Lord, and He accounted it to him for righteousness."*

Even Sarah had her doubts about bearing a child in her old age; nevertheless, she obeyed God. She did not conceive by the Holy Ghost, you know. Yes, God blessed her womb, but she had to put action behind the words that were spoken by the Lord, thereby expressing her trust and obedience to God. *"By faith Sarah herself also received strength to conceive seed, and she bore a child when she was past the age, because she judged Him faithful who had promised"* (Hebrews 11:11).

In the following verse we read that these acts of obedience had far-reaching results: *"Therefore from one man, and him as good as dead, were born as many as the stars of the sky in multitude – innumerable as the sand which is by the seashore"* (v. 12). Abraham and Sarah feared God!

The great patriarch Moses did many mighty and wondrous acts because he believed and obeyed God. Through his obedience the Israelites were released from slavery and captivity. They had every kind of need met because Moses feared the Lord!

The Bible says in Hebrews 5:7-9 about our Lord Jesus,

> Who, in the days of His flesh, when He had offered up prayers and supplications, with vehement cries and tears to Him who was able to save Him from death, and was heard because of His godly fear,
> though He was a Son, yet He learned obedience by the things which He suffered.
> And having been perfected, He became the author of eternal salvation to all who obey Him.

Think about it: Father God's desire to fellowship with His Creation once again as He did back in the Garden hinged on Jesus' obedience. The Bible says that Jesus was tempted in all things just like we are, yet He was without sin. As we read in an earlier chapter, we are not required to do anything that our forerunner Jesus didn't do also. On the other side of the coin, we are expected to do what He did, and yes, even greater works than these, according to John 14:12.

The New Testament Church gave us a starting point to proceed from. In the Acts of the Apostles we read of supernatural happenings, signs, wonders and miracles, and many believed on the Lord Jesus Christ because of what they saw.

The same book also tells us of two members of the local church whose hearts were not right before God—they lied to the Holy Spirit and dropped dead in the congregation (Acts 5). It says in verses 11 and 12 of that same chapter, *"So great fear came upon all the church and upon all who heard these things. And through the hands of the apostles many signs and wonders were done among the people. . . ."*

When the Church fears the Lord, He will be able to demonstrate His power with great signs and wonders! God desires in this day and hour to reveal Himself in all of His power and glory and majesty, and I believe the Church of the Lord Jesus Christ is getting ready for Him!

When the Church fears the Lord, He will be able to demonstrate His power with great signs and wonders!

We are clothed in His righteousness. We are walking in newness of life, in His light, and in His love. We are filled with the Spirit of God, and as we saw earlier in Isaiah 11:4, in identifying with Jesus we can now declare, ". . . with the breath of *our mouth* we shall slay the wicked. . . ." because we express exactly what God desires to express. It won't be *our* breath; it will be His breath, His Spirit.

When we walk in the light of God's Word, when we walk in the fear of the Lord, nothing contrary to that divine power will be able to stand. Every work of darkness will have to back off! Darkness cannot stand. Light overtakes darkness every time.

Those in the Body of Christ who have had a heart after God and have yearned for His manifested presence have been in a state of readiness for some time. God needs all of us in this hour. He desires for all of us to be a part of this great outpouring of His Spirit. He does not want to do without a single one of us. He has a place for every one of us in His Kingdom, but it's not a place where we fold our hands—there are no idle hands in His Kingdom.

This book has been written to help us identify, understand and apprehend the fear of the Lord. I have blown the trumpet in Zion, so to speak, and the alarm has sounded. May we all be as those wise virgins our Lord Jesus referred to who had sufficient oil in their lamps to illuminate their given spheres, putting the darkness to flight and revealing the Father's heart for mankind. Our Lord Jesus came so that we might have life and have that more abundantly. May we all be ready when the Bridegroom appears!

My prayer and confident expectation is that the light of God's Word will illuminate our understanding, and that Holy Spirit will draw us even closer to Father God and to His Son, our Savior and Lord, Jesus Christ.

The Scriptures list many rewards of fearing the Lord and will bless and encourage you to go on with God, to run the race that is set before you with patience, knowing that you will receive the reward if you faint not. We look to Jesus, the author and finisher of our faith!

When you fear the Lord, you will:

1. Serve God acceptably.

Hebrews 12:28

Therefore, since we are receiving a kingdom which cannot be shaken, let us have grace, by which we may serve God acceptably with reverence and godly fear.

Psalm 89:7

God is greatly to be feared in the assembly of the saints, and to be held in reverence by all those around Him.

2. Sin not.

Exodus 20:20

And Moses said to the people, "Do not fear; for God has come to test you, and that His fear may be before you, so that you may not sin."

3. Know it is for your good.

Deuteronomy 10:12, 13

And now, Israel, what does the Lord your God require of you, but to fear the Lord your God, to walk in all His ways and to love Him, to serve the Lord your God with all your heart and with all your soul, and to keep the commandments of the Lord and His statutes which I command you today for your good?

4. Get to know the Lord's ways.

Deuteronomy 8:6

Therefore you shall keep the commandments of the Lord your God, to walk in His ways and to fear Him.

5. Have freedom from conflict.

Proverbs 16:6, 7

In mercy and truth atonement is provided for iniquity; and by the fear of the Lord one departs from evil. When a man's ways please the Lord, He makes even his enemies to be at peace with him.

2 Chronicles 17:9, 10

So they taught in Judah, and had the Book of the Law of the Lord with them; they went throughout all the cities of Judah and taught the people. And the fear of the Lord fell on all the kingdoms of the lands that were around Judah, so that they did not make war against Jehoshaphat.

6. Bear rule.

Exodus 18:21

Moreover you shall select from all the people able men, such as fear God, men of truth, hating covetousness; and place such over them to be rulers of thousands, rulers of hundreds, rulers of fifties, and rulers of tens.

2 Samuel 23:3

The God of Israel said, The Rock of Israel spoke to me; He who rules over men must be just, ruling in the fear of God.

7. Have a long life.

Deuteronomy 6:1,2

Now this is the commandment, and these are the statutes and judgments which the Lord your God has commanded to teach you, that you may observe them in the land which you are crossing over to possess, that you may fear the Lord your God, to keep all His statutes and His commandments which I command you, you and your son and your grandson, all the days of your life, and that your days may be prolonged.

Deuteronomy 6:24

And the Lord commanded us to observe all these statutes, to fear the Lord our God, for our good always, that He might preserve us alive, as it is this day.

Proverbs 9:10, 11

The fear of the Lord is the beginning of wisdom, and the knowledge of the Holy One is understanding. For by me your days will be multiplied, and years of life will be added to you.

Proverbs 10:27

The fear of the Lord prolongs days, but the years of the wicked will be shortened.

Proverbs 14:27

The fear of the Lord is a fountain of life, to turn one away from the snares of death.

Proverbs 19:23

The fear of the Lord leads to life, and he who has it will abide in satisfaction; he will not be visited with evil.

Proverbs 22:4

By humility and the fear of the Lord are riches and honor and life.

8. Have health and healing.

Proverbs 3:7, 8

Do not be wise in your own eyes; fear the Lord and depart from evil. It will be health to your flesh, and strength to your bones.

Malachi 4:2

But to you who fear My name the Sun of Righteousness shall arise with healing in His wings; and you shall go out and grow fat like stall-fed calves.

9. Be well, and so will your children.

Deuteronomy 5:29

Oh, that they had such a heart in them that they would fear Me and always keep all My commandments, that it might be well with them and with their children forever!

10. Have deliverance

2 Kings 17:38, 39

And the covenant that I have made with you, you shall not forget, nor shall you fear other gods. But the Lord your God you shall fear; and He will deliver you from the hands of all your enemies.

Psalm 33:18, 19

Behold, the eye of the Lord is on those who fear Him, on those who hope in His mercy, to deliver their soul from death, and to keep them alive in famine.

Psalm 40:1-4

I waited patiently for the Lord; and He inclined to me, and heard my cry. He also brought me up out of a horrible pit, out of the miry clay, and set my feet upon a rock, and established my steps. He has put a new song in my mouth — praise to our God; many will see it and fear, and will trust in the Lord. Blessed is that man who makes the Lord his trust....

11. Be preserved.

Exodus 9:20, [21; 25]

He who feared the word of the Lord among the servants of Pharaoh made his servants and his livestock flee to the houses. [But he who did not regard the word of the Lord left his servants and his livestock in the field. And the hail struck throughout the whole land of Egypt, all that was in the field, both man and beast; and the hail struck every herb of the field and broke every tree of the field.]

Psalm 34:7-10

The angel of the Lord encamps all around those who fear Him, and delivers them. Oh, taste and see that the Lord is good; blessed is the man who trusts in Him! Oh, fear the Lord, you His saints! There is no want to those who fear Him. The young lions lack and suffer hunger; but those who seek the Lord shall not lack any good thing.

Isaiah 59:19

So shall they fear the name of the Lord from the west, and His glory from the rising of the sun; when the enemy comes in like a flood, the Spirit of the Lord will lift up a standard against him.

Hebrews 11:7

By faith Noah, being divinely warned of things not yet seen, moved with godly fear, prepared an ark for the saving of his household, by which he condemned the world and became heir of the righteousness which is according to faith.

12. Have forgiveness.

Psalm 130:3, 4

If You, Lord, should mark iniquities, O Lord, who could stand? But there is forgiveness with You, that You may be feared.

13. Have justice.

2 Chronicles 19:5-7

Then he set judges in the land throughout all the fortified cities of Judah, city by city, and said to the judges, "Take heed to what you are doing, for you do not judge for man but for the Lord, who is with you in the judgment. Now therefore, let the fear of the Lord be upon you; take care and do it, for there is no iniquity with the Lord our God, no partiality, nor taking of bribes."

Psalm 19:9

The fear of the Lord is clean, enduring forever; the judgments of the Lord are true and righteous altogether.

14. Have success.

Joshua 1:8

This Book of the Law shall not depart from your mouth, but you shall meditate in it day and night, that you may observe to do according to all that is written in it. For then you will make your way prosperous, and then you will have good success.

Psalm 111:10

The fear of the Lord is the beginning of wisdom; a good understanding (or success) have all those who do His commandments. His praise endures forever.

15. Have wisdom and understanding.

Job 28:28

And to man He said, "Behold, the fear of the Lord, that is wisdom, and to depart from evil is understanding."

Proverbs 9:10

The fear of the Lord is the beginning of wisdom, and the knowledge of the Holy One is understanding."

Proverbs 15:33

The fear of the Lord is the instruction of wisdom, and before honor is humility.

16. Enter into true worship.

Psalm 5:7

But as for me, I will come into Your house in the multitude of Your mercy; in fear of You I will worship toward Your holy temple (lit. *the temple of Your holiness*).

Psalm 22:23

You who fear the Lord, praise Him! All you descendants of Jacob, glorify Him, and fear Him, all you offspring of Israel!

17. Know the Lord's goodness.

Psalm 31:19

Oh, how great is Your goodness, which You have laid up for those who fear You, which You have prepared for those who trust in You in the presence of the sons of men!

18. Be the friend of God.

John 15:14

You are My friends if you do whatever I command you.

19. Have your prayers answered.

Psalm 66:16-20

Come and hear, all you who fear God, and I will declare what He has done for my soul. I cried to Him with my mouth, and He was extolled with my tongue. If I regard iniquity in my heart, the Lord will not hear. But certainly God has heard me; He has attended to the voice of my prayer. Blessed be God, who has not turned away my prayer, nor His mercy from me!

20. Obtain mercy.

Psalm 103:11, 13

For as the heavens are high above the earth, so great is His mercy toward those who fear Him; As a father pities his children, so the Lord pities those who fear Him.

Psalm 103:17; 18

But the mercy of the Lord is from everlasting to everlasting on those who fear Him, and His righteousness to children's children, to such as keep His covenant, and to those who remember His commandments to do them.

Psalm 118:4-6

Let those who fear the Lord now say, "His mercy endures forever." I called on the Lord in distress; the Lord answered me and set me in a broad place. The Lord is on my side; I will not fear. What can man do to me?

Luke 1:49, 50

For He who is mighty has done great things for me, and holy

is His name. And His mercy is on those who fear Him from generation to generation.

21. Be sustained.

Psalm 111:5

He has given food to those who fear Him, He will ever be mindful of His covenant.

Proverbs 22:4

By humility and the fear of the Lord are riches and honor and life.

22. Experience salvation.

Psalm 85:9

Surely His salvation is near to those who fear Him, that glory may dwell in our land.

Acts 13:26

Men and brethren, sons of the family of Abraham, and those among you who fear God, to you the word of this salvation has been sent.

23. Know truth.

Psalm 25:14

The secret of the Lord is with those who fear Him, and He will show them His covenant.

John 7:16, 17

Jesus answered them and said, "My doctrine is not Mine, but His who sent Me. If anyone wills to do His will, he shall know concerning the doctrine, whether it is from God or whether I speak on My own authority."

24. Be blessed of the Lord.

Psalm 115:11-15

You who fear the Lord, trust in the Lord; He is their help and their shield. The Lord has been mindful of us; He will bless us; He will bless the house of Israel; He will bless the house of Aaron. He will bless those who fear the Lord, both small and great. May the Lord give you increase more and more, you and your children. May you be blessed by the Lord, who made heaven and earth.

25. Have your desires fulfilled.

Psalm 145:17-20a

The Lord is righteous in all His ways, gracious in all His works. The Lord is near to all who call upon Him, to all who call upon Him in truth. He will fulfill the desire of those who fear Him; He also will hear their cry and save them. The Lord preserves all who love Him....

26. Give God pleasure.

Psalm 147:11

The Lord takes pleasure in those who fear Him, in those who hope in His mercy.

27. Defeat the enemy.

Malachi 4:2, 3

"But to you who fear My name the Sun of Righteousness shall arise with healing in His wings; and you shall go out and grow fat like stall-fed calves. You shall trample the wicked, for they shall be ashes under the soles of your feet on the day that I do this," says the Lord of hosts.

28. Have knowledge.

Proverbs 1:7

The fear of the Lord is the beginning of knowledge....

Proverbs 2:6

For the Lord gives wisdom; from His mouth come knowledge and understanding....

John 15:15

No longer do I call you servants, for a servant does not know what his master is doing; but I have called you friends, for all things that I heard from My Father I have made known to you.

29. Have confidence.

Proverbs 14:26

In the fear of the Lord there is strong confidence, and His children will have a place of refuge.

30. Have guidance.

Psalm 25:12

Who is the man that fears the Lord? Him shall He teach in the way He chooses.

31. Have honor.

Psalm 15:1-5

Lord, who may abide in Your tabernacle? Who may dwell in Your holy hill? He who walks uprightly, and works righteousness, and speaks the truth in his heart; He who does not backbite with his tongue, nor does evil to his neighbor, nor does he take up a reproach against his friend; In whose eyes a vile person is despised, but he honors those who fear the Lord; he who swears to his own hurt and does not change; He who does not put out his money as usury, nor does he take a bribe against the innocent. He who does these things shall never be moved.

Proverbs 22:4

By humility and the fear of the Lord are riches and honor and life.

32. See signs and wonders.

Acts 2:42, 43

And they continued steadfastly in the apostles' doctrine and fellowship, in the breaking of bread, and in prayers. Then fear came upon every soul, and many wonders and signs were done through the apostles.

Acts 5:11, 12a

So great fear came upon all the church and upon all who heard these things. And through the hands of the apostles many signs and wonders were done among the people....

33. Have church growth.

Acts 9:31

Then the churches throughout all Judea, Galilee, and Samaria had peace and were edified. And walking in the fear of the Lord and in the comfort of the Holy Spirit, they were multiplied.

34. Mature in holiness.

2 Corinthians 7:1

Therefore, having these promises, beloved, let us cleanse ourselves from all filthiness of the flesh and spirit, perfecting holiness in the fear of God.

35. Receive a reward.

Colossians 3:22-24

Bondservants, obey in all things your masters according to the flesh, not with eyeservice, as men-pleasers, but in sincerity of heart, fearing God. And whatever you do, do it heartily, as to the Lord and not to men, knowing that from the Lord you will receive the reward of the inheritance; for you serve the Lord Christ.

Revelation 11:16-18

And the twenty-four elders who sat before God on their thrones fell on their faces and worshiped God, saying, "We give You thanks, O Lord God Almighty, the One who is and who was and who is to come, because You have taken Your great power and reigned. The nations were angry, and Your wrath has come, and the time of the dead, that they should be judged, and that You should reward Your servants the prophets and the saints, and those who fear Your name, small and great...."

Becoming a Child of God

Every person on this planet is a triune being. By that I mean that this being has a physical body (flesh and bones); it has a soul (mind, will and emotions); and it has a spirit which is eternal in substance. We may go through life for many years and not give any thought to God or eternity, but there comes a day in every person's life when he or she recognizes that their innermost being is being touched by their Creator God. We become aware of His great compassion for us, of His leading and guiding us. Scripture says of Jesus Christ in John 1:9 that He "...was the true Light which gives light to *every man* coming into the world."

How we respond to this divine encounter will have consequences in this life and for eternity. God wants you to choose *life* — the abundant life Jesus offers to everyone who comes to Him — to know His great love for you, to experience the joy, peace and hope found in Him alone. Jesus willingly became the sacrificial Lamb of God and shed His precious blood to atone for your sins and mine. He offers reconciliation and abundant life to all who will receive Him. ". . . *Apart from the outpouring of blood there is no remission of sins*" (Hebrews 9:22b, WNT).

> ". . . If you confess with your mouth the Lord Jesus and believe in your heart that God has raised Him from the dead, you will be saved.
> For with the heart one believes unto righteousness, and with the mouth confession is made unto salvation."
> Romans 10:9, 10

If you have felt such a stirring in your heart, don't wait any longer. Pray this with me now:

"Dear God, I need You. Thank you for loving me so much that You sent Jesus to die for me so I can be restored to the same fellowship that Adam had with You in the Garden. Thank You, God, for forgiving all of my sins and removing them as far as the East is from the West, never remembering them again. Jesus, I believe that You are the Son of God and that God raised You from the dead. I confess You as my Lord and I forsake all other gods. Jesus, come into my heart; make Your home in me and lead me every day of my life. Thank You, Father God, for adopting me into Your family. Amen."

Welcome to the family!

If you would like to write us and share with us your newly found place in God's family, we will send you a beautiful, handmade Scripture notecard as a welcome gift. Address your correspondence to:

Ekklesia Productions
P. O. Box 2150
St. Augustine, FL 32085-2150

Receiving Power From On High

After Jesus was raised from the dead, and before He ascended to the right hand of the Father, He had a number of encounters with His disciples which included the apostles and many other believers. He expounded to them things they needed to know about the Kingdom of God.

On one such occasion, Jesus gave them the following instruction:

> ". . . Wait for the Promise of the Father, which... you have heard from Me;
> "for John truly baptized with water, but you shall be baptized with the Holy Spirit not many days from now."
>
> Acts 1:4b-5

The promise Jesus refers to is found in John 14:15-18, where He is again speaking to His followers:

> "If you love Me, keep My commandments.
> And I will pray the Father, and He will give you another Helper, that He may abide with you forever—
> the Spirit of truth, whom the world cannot receive, because it neither sees Him nor knows Him; but you know Him, for He dwells with you and will be in you.
> I will not leave you orphans; I will come to you."

When we receive Jesus as our Savior, our spirit man, that eternal part deep in our belly, awakens to God. Jesus, in speaking to believers, is promising to empower them by His Spirit so that they are able to fulfill the Great Commission, radiating His presence:

> "But you shall receive power when the Holy Spirit has come upon you; and you shall be witnesses to Me in Jerusalem, and in all Judea and Samaria, and to the end of the earth."
>
> Acts 1:8

We receive power to be His witnesses, meaning we increasingly come to recognize what He has done to equip us so we can be all He has created us to be. We are enabled, by His Spirit, to give an account of His marvelous workings in our lives which will give hope and encouragement to others. We receive this power from on high so we can stand strong, not bending or breaking in the storms of life, but staying above the circumstances, looking to Jesus, the author and finisher of our faith (Hebrews 12:2).

If you would like to receive this power Jesus promised to those who believe, pray this right now:

"Dear Jesus, You are no respecter of persons. You said 2,000 years ago that Your disciples needed this power to be Your witnesses. I ask You to fill me with Your power so I can be all You have created me to be. Holy Spirit of God, I welcome You. Live big in me every day of my life. Thank You, Jesus, for filling me to overflowing. Amen."

A Prayer of Consecration

"Lord, I receive Your words and treasure Your commands within me. I incline my ear to wisdom, and apply my heart to understanding; yes, I cry out for discernment, and lift up my voice for understanding—indeed, I seek her as silver, and search for her as for hidden treasures.

"Therefore I will understand the fear of the Lord, and find the knowledge of God. For You, Lord, give wisdom; from Your mouth come knowledge and understanding; You store up sound wisdom for the upright; You are a shield to those who walk uprightly; You guard the paths of justice, and You preserve the way of Your saints. (See Proverbs 2:1-8.)

"Heavenly Father, thank You for Your Word which I receive afresh today. Jesus—Living Word, the Word made flesh—be Lord in every area of my life. Shine light on the path You have prepared for me. Save me, deliver me, keep me, protect me, heal me, and prosper me. Give me ears to hear, eyes to see, and a heart to understand. Thank You for sending Holy Spirit to help me along the way. I am so very grateful for everything You have done in my life, and I look forward to a bright tomorrow as I walk with You. Amen."

My True Identity – A Confession

God Made Me and Loves Me

- *I am God's workmanship. –Ephesians 2:10*
- *He chose me before the foundation of the world. –Ephesians 1:4*
- *Before the world was created, He loved me and chose a destiny for my life. –Ephesians 1:5*
- *Before He formed me, He knew me; before I was born, He set me apart for a unique purpose. –Jeremiah 1:5*
- *God knit me together in my mother's womb. –Psalm 139:13-17*

God Has a Plan for My Life

- *God has a good plan for my life, to prosper me and not harm me, to give me a hope and a future. –Jeremiah 29:11*
- *All my days were written in His book before one of them came to be. –Psalm 139:16*
- *God prepared good works in advance for me to do. –Ephesians 2:10*
- *God is working all things together to fulfill His good plan for me. –Romans 8:28*

Since I Have believed in Jesus, This is Who I Am:

- *I am a child of God. –John 1:12*
- *I am chosen of God, holy and dearly loved. –Colossians 3:12*
- *I am accepted. –Ephesians 1:6*
- *I am redeemed and forgiven. –Colossians 1:14*
- *I am alive with Christ. –Ephesians 2:5*
- *I am free from the law of sin and death. –Romans 8:2*

- I am holy and without blame before Him. –Ephesians 1:4
- I am free from condemnation –Romans 8:1
- I have the peace of God that passes all understanding. –Philippians 4:7
- I am a new creature in Christ. –2 Corinthians 5:17
- I am united with God and one with Him in spirit. –1 Corinthians 6:17
- I am the righteousness of God in Christ. –Philippians 3:9
- I am a temple of God. God's Spirit lives in me. –1 Corinthians 6:19
- I am complete in Jesus Christ. –Colossians 2:10
- I am seated in heavenly places with Christ. –Ephesians 2:6
- I have direct access to God. –Ephesians 2:18
- God has not given me a spirit of fear, but of love, power and a sound mind. –2 Timothy 1:7
- Nothing can separate me from His love. –Romans 8:35-39
- God will never leave me. –Hebrews 13:5
- I have the mind of Christ. –Philippians 2:5; 1 Corinthians 2:16
- I have received God's Spirit of wisdom and revelation. –Ephesians 1:17, 18
- I am a partaker of His divine nature. –2 Peter 1:3, 4
- I can do all things through Christ Who strengthens me. –Philippians 4:13
- I have power to lay hands on the sick and see them recover, to cast out demons, and to speak with new tongues. –Mark 16:17, 18
- I can quench all the fiery darts of the wicked one with my shield of faith. –Ephesians 6:16
- [Jesus has made it possible for me to do even greater works than He did.] –John 14:12
- God supplies all of my needs according to His riches in glory. –Philippians 4:19
- I am more than a conqueror through Him Who loves me. –Romans 8:37

- *I am delivered from the power of darkness and translated into God's kingdom.* –Colossians 1:13
- *I am redeemed from the curse of sin, sickness, and poverty.* –Galatians 3:13; Deuteronomy 28:1-13
- *I am healed by the stripes of Jesus.* –1 Peter 2:24; Isaiah 53:5
- *I am strengthened with all might by His glorious power.* –Colossians 1:11
- *It is not I who live, but Christ lives in me.* –Galatians 2:20
- *I am an ambassador for Christ.* –2 Corinthians 5:20
- *I am chosen to bear fruit.* –John 15:16
- *I am greatly loved by God.* –Colossians 3:12; Romans 1:7; Ephesians 2:4

For additional encouraging materials and gifts,
visit us online at:
www.ekklesiaproducts.com

Maiden Voyage Publishing Vision

*Proclaiming the living Word of God
through the power of the printed page.*

The Lord gave the word: great was the
company of those that published it.

–Psalm 68:11

www.ingramcontent.com/pod-product-compliance
Lightning Source LLC
Chambersburg PA
CBHW060836050426
42453CB00008B/713